D0210770

GAYLORD

ADVICE AND CONSENT
The Development of the Policy Sciences

ADVICE AND CONSENT
The Development of the Policy Sciences

Peter deLeon

RUSSELL SAGE FOUNDATION / NEW YORK

The Russell Sage Foundation

The Russell Sage Foundation, one of the oldest of America's general purpose foundations, was established in 1907 by Mrs. Margaret Olivia Sage for "the improvement of social and living conditions in the United States." The Foundation seeks to fulfill this mandate by fostering the development and dissemination of knowledge about the political, social, and economic problems of America. It conducts research in the social sciences and public policy, and publishes books and pamphlets that derive from this research.

The Board of Trustees is responsible for oversight and the general policies of the Foundation, while administrative direction of the program and staff is vested in the President, assisted by the officers and staff. The President bears final responsibility for the decision to publish a manuscript as a Russell Sage Foundation book. In reaching a judgment on the competence, accuracy, and objectivity of each study, the President is advised by the staff and selected expert readers. The conclusions and interpretations in Russell Sage Foundation publications are those of the authors and not of the Foundation, its Trustees, or its staff. Publication by the Foundation, therefore, does not imply endorsement of the contents of the study.

Library of Congress Cataloging-in-Publication Data

DeLeon, Peter.
  Advice and consent.

  Bibliography: p.
  Includes index.
  1. Policy sciences. 2. Political planning—United States. 3. United States—Politics and government—20th century. I. Title.
H97.D45 1988 361.6'1   88-32140
ISBN 0-87154-215-3 (alk. paper)

The paper used in this publication meets the minimum requirements of American National Standard for Information Sciences—Permanence of Paper for Printed Library Materials, ANSI Z39.48-1984.

Excerpt from "The Love Song of J. Alfred Prufrock" in *Collected Poems 1909–1962* by T. S. Eliot, copyright 1936 by Harcourt Brace Jovanovich, Inc., copyright © 1963, 1964 by T. S. Eliot, reprinted by permission of the publisher.

10 9 8 7 6 5 4 3 2 1

Preface

This monograph attempts to trace the development of an intellectual and analytic approach to address problems which are distinguished by their public policy orientation. This approach has been called "the policy sciences." Explicitly multidisciplinary, problem-oriented, and normative in outlook, their very catholicity precludes traditional academic disciplinary boundaries, perspectives, and certainly individual purviews. As I have written in *The Foundations of Policy Analysis* (with Garry D. Brewer):

> The label, *policy sciences,* was chosen carefully. *Policy* includes society's most important decisions, actions backed by widespread approval and/or threat of sanctions. *Science,* most generally, suggests means to acquire verifiable knowledge. Using science, in the plural, invites all scientific disciplines to participate while giving preference to none. Indeed, the entire label, policy sciences, was and still is an invitation to anyone concerned with both policy and science to share the distinctive frame of reference.

Under these circumstances, a certain intellectual and professional humility is in order. A more appropriate title for this monograph therefore might be *One Person's View of the Policy Sciences.*

Other caveats are equally in order. I am by inclination and discipline a historian *cum* political scientist turned policy analyst with an economist's veneer; sometimes I feel like a motherless child. I lack an eclectic knowledge of the numerous insights of sociology, the natural and physical sciences, law, and psychology, all of which have made direct contributions to the public policy issues and the policy sciences. Most of my experiences rest in American politics (and, even here, in only a limited number of issues and areas), to the sad neglect of certainly relevant available examples from other polities, societies, and times. And, lastly, I am saddled with many of the standard cultural biases and blinders (male, WASP, etc.) ascribed to the U.S. war baby generation. The following discussions will surely reveal these limitations.

In short, I cannot pretend to write the ecumenical, let alone definitive, history of the policy sciences. It is an open question if anybody could; I can speak only for myself. Nor will this be an exercise in formulating and testing a grand, overarching theory elegantly integrating the scope of the policy sciences. I trust the reader will treat the following discussion with these unfortunate but inherent limitations in mind.

While this apologia might disappoint some readers, others will, I hope, treat these admitted shortcomings as welcome opportunities. That is, the policy sciences do not represent a closed community, a restricted priesthood with incontestable covenants. For those who are interested in the policy sciences' foci and conceptual approach, this monograph can provide a foundation upon which motivated readers can apply their own knowledge to issues of importance to them without fear of violating indisputable dogma. The policy sciences have always been, are presently, and must continue to evolve as a function of their proponents' skills and concerns. As such, this particular view of the development of the policy sciences is meant to inform and inspire rather than rigidly define the past and future of the policy sciences, in terms of either subject matter or approach. Thus, rather than a rueful flaw, the very incompleteness of this discussion should be viewed as an invitation for the policy sciences' continued growth, vitality, and, most important, relevance.

Acknowledgments

As is made clear in the Preface and Introduction, this account of the development and future of the policy sciences is very much my personal view. Still, this hardly implies that it was monastically conceived. Colleagues at various research institutions, students at different universities, and any number of enlightening authors have all contributed to my understanding of what I think the policy sciences are and mean. Inevitably, some have given more than others. I would like to indulge a moment of the reader's patience and acknowledge them.

For a number of years I was a member of the research staff at the RAND Corporation, probably the most consistent quality research institution in the United States. My tenure there was tremendously educational, if not always encouraging. Specific individuals at RAND include Carl H. Builder, Bruce Goeller, Robert L. Perry, and, most of all, Albert P. Williams.

My serious thinking about American policy sciences was generated in true Henry James fashion by my limited but illuminating European experiences. West Berlin's Science Center (*Wissenschaftszentrum*) and its Director of Research Policy, Dr. Georg Thurn, were most supportive in forcing me to think less in terms of discrete analyses and more in terms of broad trends. The Swedish Council for Planning and the Coordination of Research and the Swedish Bi-Centennial Fund provided multiple opportunities for me to reflect upon American experiences as they might apply in the Swedish context. Several Europeans were instrumental in urging me to explain the policy sciences and thereby articulate what I thought were their geneses and ontogeny. Foremost among these individuals is Bjorn Wittrock (Department of Political Science, University of Stockholm), a good friend and a brilliant scholar. Others include Helga Nowotny (Department of Sociology, University of Vienna), Hellmut Wollmann (Department of Political Science, Free University of Berlin), and Mans Lonnroth (Office of the Prime Minister, Sweden).

Many colleagues at American universities warrant recognition. Although we have not always agreed, their comments have never failed to be instructive and, when merited, supportive. These include Thomas Anton (Brown), William Ascher (Duke), Eugene C. Bardach (UCB), Ronald D. Brunner (University of Colorado), P. Brett Hammond (National Academy of Sciences), Abraham Kaplan (UCLA), Martin Rein (MIT), the late John C. Ries (UCLA), and Alfred Stepan (Columbia University). Special gratitude must be accorded Garry D. Brewer (Yale University), who introduced this fledgling graduate student to the complexities of the policy sciences and served as a source of encouragement and occasional consolation ever since.

Needless to say, the Russell Sage Foundation has historically been in the vanguard of applied social science and evaluation research. It is a savored honor to join the rolls of its scholars. In candor, I would have had many of the same thoughts without the support of the Foundation but I surely would not have had the splendid opportunities generously afforded to me by the Foundation to articulate, circulate, and refine them. Specifically, I would like to acknowledge the enthusiasm of Eric Wanner (President), most particularly Peter de Janosi (Vice President), and Robert K. Merton (Resident Scholar). The assistance generously offered by the Foundation's publication staff, especially Priscilla Lewis (Director of Publications) and Charlotte Shelby (Managing Editor), has been supportive far in excess of its professional responsibility. As part of its support, the Foundation commissioned three anonymous reviews of the draft manuscript. These readers' suggestions substantially improved the final product in terms of both conceptual clarity and substantive examples. I am clearly grateful.

However influential these people and institutions might have been, I think they will understand when I reserve my most appreciative comments for Harold D. Lasswell. I was never a formal student of his; our meetings were only few and late in his life. But nevertheless, combined with his writings (which I confess to this day I have not completely read or digested), he has been, as Brewer and I set down in our dedication to *The Foundations of Policy Analysis,* a constant counselor and inspiration. I am certain that he would not be totally pleased with everything that follows, but I trust he would approve of the effort, for it is very much in his light that I approach the policy sciences.

Having rubbed such stellar elbows, one could hardly go wrong or at least lack an exculpatory finger to point. Alas: the wages of responsibility insist that I now must, of course, absolve them individually and collectively of any errors of fact, logic, interpretation, or conclusion which might follow. Such sins are traditionally the sole domain of the author. And tradition, as Tevye tells us, is what keeps the fiddler on the roof.

PETER DELEON

Contents

1 / Introduction

And we are here as on a darkling plain
Swept with confused alarms of struggle and flight,
Where ignorant armies clash by night.

—Matthew Arnold
"Dover Beach"

THE PROBLEM

The conceptual, intellectual, and professional underpinning of the policy sciences have been well articulated since at least 1951 when Lerner and Lasswell first coined the phrase and offered working definitions which remain touchstones to this day.[1] Since then, the number of proponents and practitioners of the policy sciences has grown almost geometrically, although some might claim disproportionally in terms of value and product. Numerous "market tests" manifest this growth and apparent acceptance. Virtually every major university has a training program in public policy analysis, and it is the rare governmental unit that does not have its own analytic group or ready access to such capabilities. The question facing the policy sciences, then, is not so much one of survival, but survival in what form and in what directions. That is, what shape and merit will the policy sciences assume as they transition from academic fancy to institutional fact? Moreover, what changes must be undertaken if the policy sciences are to be considered a legitimate and respected discipline rather than a helter-skelter collage of ad hoc methodologies suitable only for particular, idiosyncratic analyses? Finally, what challenges must they confront to overcome the most damaging (and contradictory) charges currently lodged against them, either haughty irrelevance or spineless pandering? In short, what is the destiny of the policy sciences and, more concretely, how can we as policy scientists affect that fate?

For two reasons, these straightforward questions cannot—indeed, should not—be blithely answered. The first reason is that they are not easily answered. Throughout their incubation and maturation, the policy sciences have deliberately sought out issues of the most intractable nature and lashed themselves to the highest normative and epistemological standards. The arms race, social welfare, energy policy, environmental disputes, and health issues are examples of subjects which illustrate the breadth and difficulty of the policy sciences' movement. As if this were not enough, the task of the policy sciences, as defined by Lasswell and Kaplan, is to provide "intelligence pertinent to the integration of values realized by and embodied in interpersonal relations," which "prizes not the glory of a depersonalized state or the efficiency of a social mechanism, but human dignity and the realization of human capacities."[2] Surely no easy charges.

The policy sciences, whatever their internal disputes, have rarely wavered from this lodestar concern with fundamental societal issues and basic values postures. One cannot understand the civil rights movements or social welfare transfer policies without a clear appreciation of their underlying normative preferences: namely, that all persons should have equal opportunity regardless of their race, creed, sex, or religion. Environmental disputes show similar bases and cleavages. This is not to claim that knowledge of opposing value positions results in amiable policy resolutions. Understanding of the other's claims has not reduced the acrimony between the pro- and anti-abortion camps; as Robinson points out, protagonists in the energy disputes scarcely speak the same language,[3] and Thompson argues that they might even emanate from different cultures.[4] This last topic is a particularly striking example since the physical reserves of petroleum or the generation of electricity should seemingly be amenable to objective quantification and policy recommendation, yet this has proven not to be the case. The point remains: the policy sciences have consciously directed themselves to addressing the most difficult problems facing society.

This is not to argue that the policy sciences are consciously or inherently Sisyphean or its practitioners masochists, just that they deliberately deal with problems that have scant pretention to easy solution. This hallmark thus obscures the answer to the question of whither the policy sciences, for there are few easy avenues if the policy sciences hold true to their original mandates. Yeats' 1920 poetic vision is apropos:

> And what rough beast, its hour come round at last,
> Slouches towards Bethlehem to be born?[5]

The second question, not totally divorced from the first, is what are the proper means to these ill-defined ends? The answers to this question can be just as perplexing as those ascribed to the first set of concerns. The "conventional" means (e.g., cost-benefit analyses and management information systems) have already been employed and, in some cases, discarded except for use in a few circumscribed instances. Most analysts are aware of the strengths, limitations, and appropriate applications of various approaches offered by organization theory, economics, political science, operations research, and social psychology, even if they might be loathe to abandon them to multidisciplinary analytic enterprises.[6] It is the synergetic syntheses of these and new approaches which must be thoughtfully melded if the full contextual complexity of contemporary issues is to be successfully encompassed. But, again, these observations on their components do little to clarify the future of the policy sciences.

Lacking convincing responses to this challenge, the policy sciences would continue to operate under the damning shadow of practical irrelevance[7] and be utilized as little more than cosmetic support for decisions and policies already chosen. The complete lack of analysis prior to President Reagan's March 1983 announcement of his profoundly important (and expensive) Strategic Defense Initiative gives substance to this rueful possibility.[8] Specific examples can be cited of methodological requirements and possibilities. If values are central to policy analysis, how can they be explicitly incorporated?[9] Who are the "instructors" and the "students"? That is, who is doing the "learning," an arguable and critical differentiation for a profession in which scholar and practitioner roles are often indistinct and interchangeable. Can risk analysis, as one example among many methodological candidates, play a contributory role?[10] Since the chosen approaches directly influence the proffered recommendations and ultimate value of the research to the public good, the answer to this set of questions will likewise be decisive in the future of the policy sciences.[11]

If one thing is certain about the yet-to-be, it is its assured uncertainties. Given the opaqueness of the future, how can we best describe and meet the challenges confronting the policy sciences in terms of their disciplinary growth, the approaches used, and the issues they will undertake? Setting cavalier speculation aside, we would best equip ourselves for such forecasting and molding by understanding the heritage, the evolution, of the policy sciences as we know and apply them today. This knowledge will at least give their practitioners a common basis for extrapolating future developments of the discipline in a contextual setting.

Therefore, understanding the discipline is central to our task, but it is not a forthright exercise. As noted above, the conceptual underpinnings of the policy sciences approach have been in hand (if not in heart) since the early 1950s. But like any newly emergent discipline, its track has been less than true in any linear sense of the term. Divergences rather than direction—meanderings in lieu of milestones—have marked its travels and travails. Its sporadic intellectual growth has seemingly been diverted, diffused, and perhaps subverted by a number of factors that have deflected it from the original goals and objectives and purposes that Lasswell, Dror,[12] and others foresaw. Successive editors of the bellwether journal *Policy Sciences* have commented on how this lack of continuity, exacerbated by changing issue landscapes, has threatened or maybe even deprived the policy sciences of their founding birthright and vision.[13] As the Cheshire Cat advised Alice as she wandered through Wonderland, if you don't know where you're going, "then it doesn't matter which way you go."

There is some argument that this condition not only should be expected but perhaps is even salutary, a normal progression that one might predict from a new discipline attempting to carve its identity out of shifting intellectual and topical environments. If previous approaches or disciplines could encompass and resolve the perceived problems, there would be little need for such fumbling explorations; Copernicus would have never been persecuted had Ptolemaic astronomy accurately described the movements of the solar system, and Einstein would have remained an obscure patents clerk if Newtonian physics had withstood the tests of relativity. But, at base, this is a self-serving bromide for policy researchers whose long-term visions are uncertain or ambivalent. As the philosophers of science and the sociologists of knowledge document, the accretion of knowledge necessary to structure and communicate a discipline must accumulate around a shared analytic framework.[14] Lacking that, one has a disparate set of observations with little connection or overarching coherence; there is, in point of epistemological fact, no discipline. Hence, there can be scant chance for advancement. The ad hoc insights policy researchers might often reach can be criticized for a lack of underlying theory, for little empirical rigor, or, most tellingly, as politically sophistic (i.e., irrelevant and therefore valueless). For a discipline that defines and prides itself in terms of relevance and real world application, these charges, if true, would be fatal. Gulliver's descriptions of the policy research undertaken by the Grand Academy of Lagado are still instructive in this regard:

> In the school of political projectors I was but ill entertained, the professors appearing in my judgment wholly out of their senses, which is a scene that never fails to make me melancholy. These unhappy people were proposing schemes for persuading monarchs to choose favourites upon the score of their wisdom, capacity, and virtue; of teaching ministers to consult the public good; . . . with many other wild impossible chimeras, that never entered before into the heart of man to conceive, and confirmed in me the old observation, that there is nothing so extravagant and irrational which some philosophers have not maintained for truth.[15]

These criticisms are, of course, neither irrelevant nor misplaced. There should be little doubt that the aggregation of societally relevant knowledge and its application to public policy issues is a difficult task,[16] many times even a thankless one. In the words of one representative federal bureaucrat, " 'We might as well be candid: Federal program evaluations so far have been largely ineffective.' O.M.B. officials also report that evaluations, by and large, have not been timely, relevant, or accessible."[17] To ask policy scientists to assume the additional burden of developing underlying integrating themes is perhaps unreasonable, not because it is unnecessary but because it adds a distracting, possibly insoluble problem to the already formidable complexities of knowledge utilization in the public policy arena. Indeed, Ascher argues:

> The policy scientist's acknowledgment of a broader base of variations in actors' motivations and behaviors results in far greater skepticism regarding the ability to formulate explicit, generalizable models. . . . The policy sciences' approach provides a general framework for cataloguing, identifying, and exploring the implication of multiple objectives, but to be applied in specific instances rather than general laws.[18]

In such a fluid environment, one should expect to find what Polanyi had called "tacit" knowledge, that is, knowledge acquired through practice that is difficult to articulate or document articulately.[19] Lindblom and Cohen refer to this as "ordinary knowledge" and claim that it is far more effective in terms of affecting policy decisions than knowledge derived from "professional [i.e., analytic] social inquiry."[20] Even if the distinction were valid and could be maintained (assumptions Emmert points out are at best worrisome and at root unnecessary),[21] this rationale, however reasonable, does not persuasively excuse the policy sciences from advancing from a feuilleton of topicality to a respected discipline of societally relevant and effective knowledge. A sorting out and stocktaking is necessary lest an intellectual sclerosis invade and disable the policy sciences.

Finally, this review is motivated by two assumptions: opportunity and imperative. The opportunity assumption is that the policy sciences as enunciated can make a difference in relieving social maladies and achieving consensual social goals. In Nathan's pithy advocacy, they "can be useful and used."[22] The imperative assumption is that it is almost certain that social ills, if left unattended, are not homeostatic or self-correcting. They will not graciously and equitably resolve themselves as a matter of course or courtesy; there is no "hidden hand" benevolently guiding public policy or alleviating injustices. More troublesome is the observation that many attendant policies might actually be counterproductive and worsen the very situations they were formulated and implemented to correct. There is evidence that drug education programs increase rather than reduce drug use in the target populations.[23] Murray proposes that the Great Society's social welfare programs have resulted in black Americans "losing ground" in their search for racial equality.[24] If the costs of inaction and neglect increase the costs of curing, then this examination of the policy sciences' potential is past due.

Thus, to reiterate, one needs to ask what has motivated and shaped the growth of the policy sciences. What trends and conditions have influenced their development as both a discipline and a profession? And, further, how might one predict, guide, and perhaps even overcome the "market forces" that have heretofore shaped the amorphous body of the policy sciences?

THE APPROACH

This monograph proposes to investigate the development of the policy sciences and their determinants by employing a Lasswellian framework.[25] This framework has two advantages. First, it has a certain internal cohesion which permits one to examine the policy sciences approach to social problems in a contextually rich yet structured manner. Second, it permits one to project future developments and ask what influence they might have. We are then, in essence, turning the policy sciences spotlight upon the policy sciences themselves to identify both their founts and futures, asking what they have done and what they might do.

At this point, it would be useful to provide some definitions. "Policy sciences," as used here, is an umbrella term describing a broad-gauge intellectual approach applied to the examination of societally critical problems. In Lasswell's terms, "The policy [sciences] approach does not imply that energy is to be dissipated on a miscellany of merely topical issues, but rather that fundamental and often neglected problems which arise in the adjustment of man in society are to be dealt with."[26] The policy sciences, as we shall see, are problem-oriented and contextual in nature, multidisciplinary in approach, and explicitly normative in perspective. They represent a variety of approaches to understanding and resolving issues of great public importance. As an explicit part of this charter, they include the ideological and value components which are an integral and operational part of politics and the political process. The policy sciences approaches necessarily encompass much more than the traditional applied social sciences because many contemporary policy problems involve critical components of the natural and physical sciences and new technologies.

"Policy analysis" is the most noted derivative and application of the tools and methodologies of the policy sciences' approach. In Dunn's words, policy analysis is "an applied social science discipline which uses multiple methods of inquiry and argument to produce and transform policy-relevant information that may be utilized in political settings to resolve policy problems."[27] Although there is some debate as to what precisely defines a policy problem,[28] policy analysis is generally considered a more discrete *genus* under the broader umbrella of the policy sciences *phylum*.[29] Quite often and unfortunately, they are used interchangeably. Similarly, "systems analysis," which many proponents claim to be synonymous with policy analysis, is even more a set of specific tools and applications, usually quantitative in nature. Systems analysis is more limited in what it encompasses and, subsequently, is able to address.[30] Within these broad categories, distinguished primarily by their investigations and purviews, there are a series of methodological tools, such as decision analysis, cost-benefit analysis, econometric modeling, and survey research.

Finally, many policy scholars focus on the "policy process" or "policy cycle" as a vehicle for explaining in general how policies are conceived, chosen, executed, and evaluated.[31] These multiple perspectives can be viewed as consonant, but should not be taken as identical. This represents a framework for placing the policy sciences' approaches in the operating political arenas. The juxtaposed policy process emphasis reflects Lasswell's early admonishment to focus on both "knowledge *of* the policy process and knowledge *in* the process."[32] We will examine the policy process more closely in later chapters. However, it is important to note here that the policy sciences have drawn upon a number of policy decisionmaking models and the overall policy process as a medium for making their research and recommendations more relevant to the problem at hand. These models are descriptively and procedurally richer than those usually found in political science and sociology because policy scientists require a clear understanding of how the policy process operates if their recommendations are to be effectively posed and utilized. To appreciate, let alone engage in, the policy symphony, one needs to interpret and manipulate both the score and the orchestration.

The basic theme of this monograph is that the evolution of the policy sciences can best be understood if one treats it as having been shaped by two separate but related sets of factors or conditions. The first set can be described as *endogenous*, that is, congeries of perceptions and methodologies drawn from psychology, sociology, many of the natural and physical sciences, law, political science, economics, and other contributing disciplines. The second set, or what one might term *exogenous*, is provided by real world, political events as they affected the policy sciences in terms of both the resulting choice of problems and the way in which the problems were approached. Historically, the two certainly interacted with and influenced each other, although it will be seen that too often they appeared like ships passing in the night. Still, for a successfully integrated and coherent policy science, the two must and did commingle. An economist might depict this relationship as one of "supply" (i.e., applicable tools) and "demand" (i.e., a need for these skills or a market). A more policy-oriented characterization—one adopted here—might be "advice" from the practitioner and "consent" from the policymaker. The following chapters will reflect this loosely posed paradigm.

Before beginning, the reader should be aware of two limitations of this study. First, it is based upon an unfortunate but patent set of parochialisms. Even though the general framework utilized here should be applicable across the broad range of cultures and polities, this discussion draws its illustrations almost exclusively from the American political milieu. At one time, this might have been more excusable because, for a variety of reasons, the policy sciences approach was largely an American phenomenon, as even the most cosmopolitan of the policy scholars, Yehezkel Dror, admits.[33] (Exceptions will be noted below.) This situation is certainly no longer true, if, indeed, it ever was; societally relevant knowledge is hardly an American national monopoly. Both in terms of policy-oriented scholars and research institutions (e.g., Sweden's

Secretariat for Futures Studies, the West Berlin Science Center, and Vienna's International Institute for Advanced Systems Analysis),[34] Europeans are active, visible, and valuable participants in the policy sciences.[35] For instance, personnel affiliated with the West Berlin Science Center will soon publish their review of the development of policy research in the OECD nations, which differs from the American experience in some important ways, such as the role of university professors.[36] Still, for this discussion, this limitation should be recognized. It will be returned to in the conclusion of this monograph.

The second limitation is that this study makes little attempt to inventory, document, and sort out what is "wrong" with the policy sciences (e.g., too many case studies or a babble of nomenclature) or propose a grand, unifying field theory. This is not to denigrate such efforts by others. And they, too, will be partially addressed in the concluding section. However, these are not the fundamental concerns of the exposition presented here.

Even lacking these particular facets, the ensuing discussion of the policy sciences can be enlightening. The analysis and conclusions will not preempt or dissuade Arnold's armies from their eternal clashings, but they can strive to illuminate the darkness and dispel the ignorance. In a republican democracy, one of changing and colliding coalitions, one should not hope to eliminate all competition, but one can aspire to inform the struggles as competently, consistently, and completely as possible. That is a worthy goal for the policy sciences, one which is both relevant and attainable. This might fall short of Lasswell's vision that "these intellectual operations are capable of contributing, to a remarkable degree, to the 'breakthroughs' that occur in the decision processes of history."[37] Without surrendering Lasswell's chalice, it is this more limited, still laudable objective which inspires the following discourse.

ENDNOTES

1. Daniel Lerner and Harold D. Lasswell, eds., *The Policy Sciences* (Stanford, CA: Stanford University Press, 1951).

2. Harold D. Lasswell and Abraham Kaplan, *Power and Society* (New Haven: Yale University Press, 1950), pp. xii and xxiv, respectively.
3. John Bridger Robinson, "Apples and Horned Toads: On the Framework-Determined Nature of the Energy Debate," *Policy Sciences* 15, no. 1 (November 1982): 23–45.
4. Michael Thompson, "Among the Energy Tribes: A Cultural Framework for the Analysis and Design of Energy Policy," *Policy Sciences* 17, no. 3 (November 1984): 321–339. Also see Aaron Wildavsky and Ellen Tenenbaum, *The Politics of Mistrust* (Beverly Hills, CA: Sage, 1981).
5. From William Butler Yeats, "The Second Coming."
6. See Hugh J. Miser and Edward S. Quade, eds., *Handbook of Systems Analysis: Craft Issues and Procedural Choices* (New York: Elsevier, 1987), for an enlightened discussion of the strengths and weaknesses of quantitative policy analyses.
7. Charles E. Lindblom and David K. Cohen, *Usable Knowledge: Social Science and Problem Solving* (New Haven: Yale University Press, 1979), argue that the success of "professional social inquiry" in alleviating societal problems is little better than random chance.
8. John Newhouse, "The Diplomatic Round: Summiteering," *New Yorker*, September 9, 1986, p. 50, describes the genuine astonishment that the President's speech produced in the Departments of State and Defense. Also see Peter deLeon, "The Influence of Analysis on U.S. Defense Policy," *Policy Sciences* 20, no. 2 (1987): 105–128.
9. For two views, see Aaron Wildavsky, "The Once and Future School of Public Policy," *Public Interest*, no. 79 (Spring 1985): 25–41; and Martin Rein, "Value-Critical Policy Analysis," in Daniel Callahan and Bruce Jennings, eds., *Ethics, the Social Sciences, and Policy Analysis* (New York: Plenum, 1983), chap. 5.
10. From different perspectives, positive and complementary answers are provided by Mary Douglas, *Risk Acceptability According to the Social Sciences* (New York: Russell Sage Foundation, 1985); and Bernard Fischoff et al., *Acceptable Risk* (New York: Cambridge University Press, 1981).
11. A convincing example of this duality is presented by William Ascher, "Editorial: Policy Sciences and the Economic Approach in a 'Post-Positivist' Era," *Policy Sciences* 20, no. 1 (April 1987): 3–10.
12. Harold D. Lasswell, *A Pre-View of Policy Sciences* (New York: American Elsevier, 1971); Yehezkel Dror, *Design for the Policy Sciences* and *Ventures in the Policy Sciences* (New York: American Elsevier, 1971).
13. Compare Garry D. Brewer, "The Policy Sciences Emerge: To Nurture and Structure a Discipline," *Policy Sciences* 5, no. 3 (Septem-

ber 1974): 239–244; Peter deLeon, "The Policy Sciences: The Discipline and the Profession," *Policy Sciences* 13, no. 1 (February 1981): 1–7; Ronald D. Brunner, "Integrating Knowledge and Action," *Policy Sciences* 17, no. 1 (May 1984): 3–11; and Ascher, "Editorial."

14. Thomas S. Kuhn, *The Structure of Scientific Revolutions* (Chicago: University of Chicago Press, 1970); Karl Popper, *The Logic of Scientific Discovery* (New York: Harper & Row, 1968).

15. Jonathan Swift, "A Voyage to Laputa . . . ," in *Gulliver's Travels* (1726), from Carl Van Doren, ed., *The Portable Swift* (New York: Viking Press, 1948), pp. 404–405.

16. Bjorn Wittrock, "Social Knowledge, Public Policy, and Social Betterment: A Review of Current Research on Knowledge Utilization in Policy-Making," *European Journal of Political Research* 10, no. 1 (1982): 83–89.

17. Quoted in Martin Rein and Sheldon H. White, "Can Policy Research Help Policy?" *Public Interest*, no. 49 (Fall 1977): 119–136, at 120. More substantial evidence to this thesis is in Carol Weiss, ed., *Using Social Research in Public Policy Making* (Lexington, MA: Heath, 1977).

18. Ascher, "Editorial," p. 6. Also see Albert O. Hirschman, "The Search for Paradigms as a Hindrance to Understanding," *World Politics* 22, no. 3 (April 1979): 329–343; and Abraham Kaplan, *The Conduct of Inquiry* (San Francisco: Chandler, 1964).

19. Michael Polanyi, *The Tacit Dimension* (Garden City, NY: Doubleday, 1966); and Michael Polanyi, *Personal Knowledge* (Chicago: University of Chicago Press, 1977).

20. Lindblom and Cohen, *Usable Knowledge*.

21. Mark A. Emmert, "Ordinary Knowing and Policy Science: Making Ends Meet," *Knowledge* 7, no. 1 (September 1985): 97–112.

22. Richard P. Nathan, "Research Lessons from the Great Society," *Journal of Policy Analysis and Management* 4, no. 3 (Spring 1985): 423.

23. Peter Kerr, "Experts Say Some Antidrug Efforts by Schools Harm More Than They Help," *New York Times*, September 17, 1986, pp. 1, 49.

24. Charles Murray, *Losing Ground* (New York: Basic Books, 1984).

25. The best example is Lasswell, *A Pre-View of Policy Sciences*.

26. Harold D. Lasswell, "The Policy Orientation," in Lerner and Lasswell, eds., *The Policy Sciences*, p. 14.

27. William N. Dunn, *Public Policy Analysis* (Englewood Cliffs, NJ: Prentice-Hall, 1981), p. 35. A second representative definition is Thomas R. Dye, *Understanding Public Policy* (Englewood Cliffs, NJ: Prentice-Hall, 1987), pp. 7–8.

28. See, e.g., Aaron Wildavsky, *Speaking Truth to Power: The Art and*

Craft of Policy Analysis (Boston: Little, Brown, 1979), "Introduction."

29. Garry D. Brewer and Peter deLeon, *The Foundations of Policy Analysis* (Homewood, IL: Dorsey, 1983), chap. 1.
30. Edward S. Quade, *Analysis for Public Decisions* (New York: Elsevier, 1982); and Miser and Quade, eds., *Handbook of Systems Analysis.*
31. Harold D. Lasswell, *The Decision Process* (College Park: University of Maryland Press, 1956); Brewer and deLeon, *The Foundations of Policy Analysis;* Judith May and Aaron Wildavsky, eds., *The Policy Cycle* (Beverly Hills, CA: Sage, 1978); and Randall B. Ripley, *Policy Analysis and Political Science* (Chicago: Nelson-Hall, 1985).
32. Harold D. Lasswell, "The Emerging Conception of the Policy Sciences," *Policy Sciences* 1, no. 1 (Spring 1970): 3. Emphasis in original.
33. Yehezkel Dror, *Policymaking Under Adversity* (New Brunswick, NJ: Transaction Books, 1986), suggests that the policy research and facilities are still almost exclusively Western phenomena.
34. A more complete review is Yehezkel Dror, "Required Breakthroughs in Think Tanks," *Policy Sciences* 16, no. 3 (February 1984): 199–225; at pp. 224–225.
35. For an overview, see Arnold J. Heidenheimer, "Comparative Public Policy: An Odyssey in Four Parts," *International Social Science Journal* 38, no. 2 (1986): 159–178.
36. Peter Wagner et al., eds., *Social Science in Societal Contexts: The Policy Orientation and Beyond: National Experiences in Comparative Perspective* (Cambridge: Cambridge University Press, forthcoming).
37. Harold D. Lasswell, *Politics: Who Gets What, When, How* (New York: World Publishing, 1958), p. 190. This quotation appears in a postscript prepared for the 1958 edition; *Politics* was originally written in 1936.

2 / Advice: The Policy Sciences as a Discipline

No! I am not Prince Hamlet, nor was meant to be;
Am an attendant lord, one that will do
To swell a progress, start a scene or two,
Advise the prince; no doubt, an easy tool,
Deferential, glad to be of use.
Politic, cautious, and meticulous;
Full of high sentence, but a bit obtuse;

—T. S. Eliot
"The Love Song of J. Alfred Prufrock"

A HISTORICAL BACKDROP

Policy analysis and its consequent advice have been practiced in one form or another since people have been making decisions that have policy implications, virtually since the serpent hissed in Eve's receptive ear. Dunn proposes that

> the earliest recorded examples of conscious efforts to analyze public policy are found in Mesopotamia. The ancient Mesopotamian city of Ur . . . produced one of the first legal codes in the twenty-first century B.C., some two thousand years before Aristotle (384–322 B.C.), Confucius (551–479 B.C.), and Kautilya (circa 300 B.C.) produced their classic treatises on government and politics. The Code of Hammurabi, written by the ruler of Babylon in the eighteenth century B.C., expresses a need to establish a unified and just public order in a period when Babylon was in transition from a small city-state to a large territorial state.[1]

Barbara Tuchman recreates a debate among the leaders of Troy as to whether or not to accept the Greek-proffered Trojan Horse as an early example—and failure—of policy analysis.[2] Policy analysis as a political exercise, then, is hardly a new or novel idea.

14

Still, historically, policy analysis and advice were very per-sonalized, idiosyncratic activities, passing from sage to ruler, from counselor to monarch, with only scarce and episodic regard for recording and routinizing the activity.[3] These were, in fact, zeal-ously protected prerogatives; their practitioners had little incen-tive to share their closely guarded secrets or access. The oracle at Delphi, even with its organized priesthood and famed forecasting powers, left little record of its divinations.[4]

Systematic, continuous policy counsel probably grew out of the church and state relationship, especially in western Europe, or possibly at a later date, as a temporal reaction against the church's involvement in the affairs of state. Like so many themes in West-ern civilization, it was not until the Italian Renaissance that policy advice assumed a more institutionalized basis, the writings of Machiavelli being only the most celebrated illustration. More's *Utopia* (1516) academy provided a haven for social contemplation; Bacon's *New Atlantis* (1627) applied scientific knowledge to the circles of government; by the time of Swift, policy advice was sufficiently entrenched to be satirized by the deliberations of the Academy of Projectors in Gulliver's voyage to Lagado (1726). The worldly philosophers such as Erasmus and the English political philosophers (e.g., Locke and Hobbes) set the intellectual tone for the subsequent study of politics and administration which are generally held to be the partial precursors of the policy sciences.

What was important in this historical progression was the growing political acceptance of knowledge that was apparently of use or value to those with ruling responsibilities, a condition reflected by the influence of the eighteenth-century British polit-ical philosophers (such as Burke, Bentham, and Hume) and their continental contemporaries. The increased involvement and in-teraction of political philosophy with political events was explo-sively manifested during the Age of Revolution by the French *philosophes* (e.g., Montesquieu's *The Spirit of Laws* [1748] and Rous-seau's *Social Contract* [1762]), and, most pointedly, Paine's exhor-tations to rebellion. *The Federalist Papers* (1787–1788) elaborated upon the interplay of political doctrine with specific ideas as to how a government should be structured and operate. The later Age of Ideology aggressively expanded this trend. "Academics" (broadly defined) were accorded their day in court, however infrequent or erratic those agenda might be.

However, while there might have been an apparent recognition of the need for nominally independent policy advice routinely offered to governing bodies, this counsel was realistically tendered on a parochial, personalized, and circumstantial basis, largely predicated upon political caprice, expediency, acquaintance, and, most of all, sycophancy.[5] On the other side of the policy advice coin, the political philosophers were far from objective counselers or detached participants. There was little consideration of intellectual underpinnings, honesty, cumulative knowledge, or independent evaluations as they could be applied to policy issues, even though political conditions might have been directly addressed. In short, there was little reason for these activities to pretend to the trappings of the policy *sciences* (not unlike the contributions of astrology to astronomy), even in their most inchoate form. They did provide an intellectual stimulus and some practical precedents to the later development and articulation of societally relevant knowledge. Still, from an institutional perspective, policy advice remained very particularistic, ad hoc exercises.

Even in the exceedingly cosmopolitan European court settings of the eighteenth and early nineteenth centuries, one monarch's advisers were rarely another's (although there were some spectacular exceptions, such as Talleyrand and Metternich). There was little conception of a policy process or what composed a good policy; certainly there was no explicit research or literature to these issues. As a point of historical record, few inklings of the disciplinary contributions and social consciences which would later define the policy sciences approach are to be found.

The growth of applied empirical research in France and England during the nineteenth century coincided with public awareness of acute social problems.[6] Social scientists began to train their disciplinary tools upon various perceived social maladies. Descriptive statistics were used to plot the magnitude and plight of the burgeoning urban destitute population and, in Sweden, the emigration problem. The initial emergence of ameliorative forms of empirical social research was seen as

> early modern social science responded in large part to the knowledge needs of the state, as is perhaps best indicated by some of the names under which it made its appearance: "statistics," "police

science," and "Staatswissenschaft." In fact, the shift from a largely normative and philosophical approach to society to one grounded in factual knowledge is probably the most important intellectual correlate of the rise of the modern state.[7]

No doubt the prevailing political and social conditions could have benefited from concerted and sustained policy research. The English Industrial Revolution produced strident demands for social welfare programs, just as the American Progressive movements placed insistent stresses on state and then federal governments. While new policies were initiated to relieve these tensions, they certainly were not brought about by analytic examinations of the conditions and trends. Examples of early research towards the documentation and alleviation of social woes were not totally lacking, but were generally isolated and nonrecurring.[8] Dickens and Shaw were probably more influential in affecting British social welfare legislation than Booth and the Webbs, just as the muckrakings of the Tarbells and Sinclairs stoked the political fires of the American Progressive movements.

There were some unquestionably important developments in the academic disciplines. Economics were beginning to mature as a set of possible insights into policy issues; Adam Smith's writing in political economy and David Ricardo's influence on English agriculture and free trade policies are the most prominent examples. Historians, of course, were in the vanguard in contextual studies, but their works were largely descriptive and retrospective in thrust and tone; they almost never assumed a prescriptive or even contemporary perspective. Therefore, it is not surprising that history (as a discipline as opposed to individual historians) had little to contribute to public debates. Just as important as the fledgling applications in economics and sociology was the emergence of science as a social phenomenon. The principal intellectual motif of the late nineteenth century was that social laws akin to physical and natural counterparts could be discovered and applied. Social Darwinism—as interpreted by Herbert Spencer and T. H. Huxley—was a strain consistently orchestrated on both sides of the Atlantic. The influence of the pragmatic and positivist philosophers, best articulated by the Americans William James and John Dewey,[9] was to have a profound effect on the later development of the policy sciences, for it was their thesis that rational, scientific advice and procedures could and should have a direct effect on social problems. Marxian dialectics surely had societal implications and applications. Lastly, the study of politics was starting to define itself in matters pertaining to issues of governance, which led to the study of administration. Max Weber, although formally trained as a sociologist, was the conceptual titan in this endeavor.[10] In summary, the academic disciplines were beginning to forage (albeit timidly) beyond the cloistered groves of academe and wonder if they had a role in the larger social environment, that is, to test cautiously the notion of societally relevant knowledge.

Thus, even though the systematic and routinized examination of public policy issues and problems was not in existence by the start of the twentieth century—certainly not from an organized, institutional basis—many of the disciplinary contributions which would later emerge as central components of and stimuli to the policy sciences were starting to fall into place as attractive participants. It is key, however, to note here that these various approaches were developing their limited policy concerns and insights in isolation from one another, that they were largely fixated on defining themselves as separate and very differentiated disciplines rather than coordinated, integrated approaches to contextual social problems. Indeed, as these disciplines struggled for their respective, distinctive identities, they adopted intellectual boundaries which jealously precluded other perspectives. For instance, the successors to Smith's political economy virtually neglected its political aspects as economists moved to make their field more pristine and "scientific," i.e., exclusionary. This trend was to continue well into the following century.

THE TWENTIETH CENTURY

To understand the growth of the policy sciences in the twentieth century, it is useful to abandon the relatively chronological narrative that has brought us to this point. In its stead, we can trace their development in the three principal defining characteristics of the policy sciences approach as set forth by Lasswell:[11]

- multidisciplinary in approach
- problem-oriented and contextual in nature
- explicitly normative in perspective

In many ways, these characteristics represent different levels of analysis, for they reflect distinct events and conditions. In other ways, they can be viewed as mutually reinforcing, as they were intended to be. For purposes of the present exposition and at the risk of some redundancy, they will be discussed individually because each has had an identifiable influence on the evolution and acceptance of the policy sciences.

Multidisciplinary in Approach

By the late 1920s, European sociologists of knowledge, particularly Karl Mannheim, were beginning to urge their colleagues to bring their respective expertise and knowledge to bear on social problems. Mannheim wrote that "history, statistics, political theory, sociology, history of ideas, and social psychology, among many other disciplines, represent fields of knowledge important to political leaders."[12] American political scientist Charles Merriam was even more farsighted in his 1925 presidential *tour de force* before the American Political Science Association:

> Likewise we are likely to see a closer integration of the social sciences themselves, which in the necessary process of differentiation have in many cases become too isolated. In dealing with basic problems such as those of the punishment and prevention of crime, alcoholism, the vexed question of human migration, the relations of the negro, and a wide variety of industrial and agricultural problems, it becomes evident that neither the facts and the technique of economics alone, nor of politics alone, nor of history alone, are adequate to their analysis and interpretation. . . .
> After all, it does not seriously matter what this integration is called, whether sociology or *staatswissenschaft* or anthropology or economics or politics. The essential consideration is that the point of view and the contacts are obtained and sustained in the various fields of social inquiry; that partial treatment does not twist and warp the judgment of social observers and analysts. The problem of social behavior is essentially one problem, and while the angles of the approach may and should be different, the scientific result will be imperfect unless these points of view are at times brought together in some effective way, so that the full benefit of the multiple analysis may be realized.[13]

However prescient Mannheim and Merriam might have been in their 1920s assaults on disciplinary satraps and appeals for applied social science research, their pleas fell largely on fallow ground. No university departments or professional associations snatched up the gauntlets dropped by Mannheim and Merriam. They might have been too busy consolidating and protecting their own professional identities and egos; they might have been too enamored with the hallowed academic tradition of independence (some might say isolation) from their surrounding communities, be they social or professional. As Manicas later summarized the academic tenor of the times:

> Why should social problems be less subject to scientific solutions than any other problems? But if social scientists were to be professionals with legitimate claims to authority and autonomy, they must mark out their own scientific territory and establish their own systems of credentialing. It was clear to them what this meant: they must constitute disciplines, deliberately and systematically, in exactly the manner in which everyone said natural science was constituted.[14]

Whatever the exact reasons, although certainly there were intellectual refinements during the 1920s and 1930s, most were directed internally towards methodological enhancements rather than externally towards community problems and other disciplinary perspectives. Political science, for example, was becoming embroiled in the behavioral debate, one that both threatened the internal cohesion of the field and truncated its communications to other disciplines. Economics, for another, was thoroughly enmeshed in the web of numbing empiricism, to the serious detriment of its view of the functioning economic world. The emerging field of public administration—one consciously dedicated to serving and improving the practice of government—was practically emasculated by its internal squabbles over scientific versus humanistic management (e.g., Taylor versus Bernard) and the "objective" role of the bureaucrat as an instrument of government.[15]

One can cite individual and institutional exceptions: sociologist Robert Merton,[16] economist Wesley Mitchell,[17] the establishment of the Social Science Research Council (incorporated in 1923 under Merriam's tutelage and the sponsorship of the Rockefeller foundations)[18] and the consolidation of the Brookings Institution (in 1928 with assistance from the Carnegie Foundation)[19] come prominently to mind. However, these exceptions were so strikingly out of character as to support the generality that multidisciplinary research and its applications to social problems was an unequal battle between the isolated few and the well-entrenched status quo.[20]

Thus, it is not surprising that in 1939 Robert Lynd would pose the profoundly basic and embarrassing question to his university colleagues: Knowledge for what?, asking what was the place of social science in the American culture. Railing against what he viewed as excessive empiricism (including the work of Mitchell) and social detachment, he cautioned that "if the social scientist is too bent upon 'waiting until all the data are in' . . . the decisions will be made anyway—without him . . . by the 'practical' man and by the 'hard-headed' politician chivvied by interest-pressure bloc."[21] What then, asked Lynd, was the ultimate purpose of knowledge—for its own sake or to better society? The answer was patent in most academic circles: the repute, the very idea of societally relevant knowledge was in deliberate neglect, if not outright rejection. The situation was to remain largely intact until the end of World War II, as American intellectual resources were mobilized to the exigencies at hand.

Immediately after the war, Congress and the executive sought to define the government sponsorship of scientific research as an instrument of public policy. The issue was heated as Congress debated the creation and purview of what was to become the National Science Foundation (NSF);[22] many of the same issues also surfaced in the hearings which led to the legislation creating the Atomic Energy Commission.[23] The downtrodden position of the social (compared with the physical) sciences was highlighted during the NSF deliberations; they were congressionally excluded from the foundation's sponsorship when the NSF was finally mandated in 1950. As Senator William Fulbright commented during the hearings, "People simply don't appreciate the significance of social sciences, which means your legislators don't either."[24] This attitude hardly boded well for the development of the policy sciences, which might have had a claim on the issue of relevance but had no organized stakeholders or spokespersons to articulate, let alone advance, their case.

There were, however, key pioneers and proponents willing to

span academic disciplines and argue forcefully for the necessary application of multidisciplinary research to social problems. Merton, in his landmark 1949 "Research Memorandum," called for an " 'applied social research on applied social research' to ferret out the public images of social science, particularly among makers of policy in government, labor and business." Asserting that it was "well-known, a given practical problem requires the *collaborative* researches of several social sciences," Merton stated that "practical problems are many faceted. They can be examined from the perspectives of several different disciplines." He singled out anthropology, psychology, social psychology, and sociology as especially relevant. Merton challenged social scientists to "sensitize policy-makers to new types of achievable goals . . . [and] to more effective means of reaching established goals." He concluded that "a major function of applied research is to provide occasion and pressures for inter-disciplinary investigations and for the development of a theoretic system of 'basic social science,' rather than discrete bodies of uncoordinated specialized theory."[25]

The second major proponent of the need for multidisciplinary research was Lasswell, as set forth in the first of his seminal contributions directly addressed to the policy sciences, "The Policy Orientation" (1951). His admonitions were immediately policy-directed in nature and multidisciplinary in execution:

> A policy orientation has been developing that cuts across the existing specializations. The orientation is twofold. In part it is directed towards the policy process, and in part towards the intelligence needs of policy. The first task, which is the development of a science of policy forming and execution, uses the methods of social and psychological inquiry. The second task, which is the improving of the concrete content of the information and the interpretations available to policy-makers, typically goes outside the boundaries of social science and psychology.

After emphasizing recent progress in psychology and psychometrics, Lasswell noted that the "policy sciences" were not to be equated with "applied social science" or "applied social and psychological science." "Nor," he cautioned, "are the 'policy sciences' to be thought of as largely identical with what is studied by the 'political scientists.' " Dedicated to the "fuller realization of human dignity," "the basic emphasis of the approach . . . is upon the fundamental problems of man in society. . . ." Finally, after arguing for a more intimate relationship between the potential adviser and the policy process, Lasswell advised that "in order to bring the academician and the active policy-maker into fruitful association, new institutions are needed. . . ."[26]

It is instructive to pause and examine Lasswell's vision of the policy sciences as a microcosm of the discipline's multidisciplinary touchstone. He was formally educated as a political scientist under the supervision of Merriam. This almost surely gives root to his calls for social activism within the political science profession.[27] His early interest and training in psychiatry[28] manifested itself in his conception of the policy sciences as a contextual, introspective endeavor. As Torgerson observes: "The project of contextual orientation conceived by Lasswell is highly ambitious because it seeks a knowledge of the *whole;* at the same time, it is rather modest because it does not expect complete success."[29] Lasswell's respect for the legal aspects of policy was reflected by his long-time and close association with lawyer Myres McDougal and the Yale University School of Law.[30] His exposure to Marxism resulted in his emphasis on "configurative analysis" and "developmental constructs" as "aids in the total task of clarifying goals, noting trends, and estimating future possibilities,"[31] tasks which Lasswell later defined as key elements to the policy sciences approach.[32] Lastly, and probably in the forefront of Lasswell's mind at this time, was his interest in linguistics, propaganda, and political symbols, all of which had been his immediate concern during his wartime work at the Library of Congress.[33] The breadth of Lasswell's knowledge is impressive by any standard.[34] That he was able to bring much of it to bear on what his perception of what the policy sciences could and should be reveals a great deal regarding their multidisciplinary character.

Like Merriam's and Mannheim's earlier proposed agenda, however, the scenarios laid down by Merton, Lasswell, and other early advocates of the policy sciences approach seemingly were performed without an audience or, perhaps even more discouraging, those in the audience sat on their collective hands. Except for a rare review of the Lerner-Lasswell volume,[35] contemporary academicians were apparently just as oblivious to the message as their interbellum counterparts. The obvious audience should have been political scientists, but they were internally rent by the behavioral conflicts and had little time, inclination, or resources to adopt a new disciplinary focus.[36] Many years and reflections later, Lasswell was asked how he might explain this neglect; he responded somewhat ambiguously, "I guess the times just were not right."[37] The disciplinary contributions to the policy sciences movement remained basically dormant until the late 1950s and early 1960s.

Two major disciplinary contributors—operations researchers and, a short time later, economists—were to move aggressively into this void. Arguably, Lineberry claims the cradle of policy sciences lies within economics, not political science, and cites Koopmans' "efforts during World War II to develop a theory of resource allocation" as the discipline's genesis were he asked to "locate the origins of policy sciences . . . with a person and place."[38] Operations research, in the guise of systems analysis, advanced its methodological tools to a series of discrete problems with some noted successes. Even though the more cognizant systems analysts generally limited the scope of their work to relatively limited problems, the equating of systems analysis and policy analysis remained in much of the literature; in 1980, Majone and Quade, certainly two of the most astute systems analysts, wrote that "systems analysis and policy analysis are used as essentially synonymous terms for the same activity."[39]

More than likely, the emergence and dominance of these more quantitative approaches to public policy issues was a reaction against the more amorphous and removed types of analysis produced by political scientists and the ineffective efforts of public administration to improve governmental processes and services. At the same time, it was a function of the successes that systems and cost-benefit analyses and economics were enjoying in certain sectors of government in the United States, especially in the Department of Defense.[40] Although the more perceptive practitioners always warned of the limitations of such methodologies, cost-benefit analysis, systems analysis, Program Planning Budgeting System (PPBS), and quantitative modeling became prevalent passwords for policy analysis—for example, Quade and Boucher's *Systems Analysis and Policy Planning*.[41] In many instances, analysis was replaced by technique; the "need" to quantify, to reduce all policies to a set of economic or quantitative indicators seemingly became pervasive. Analytic techniques and procedures the defense realm extended to social issues were not long in coming; e.g., in 1965, President Lyndon Johnson ordered PPBS as practiced in the Department of Defense to be instituted in the Department of Health, Education, and Welfare. However limiting or even detrimental these blinders might have been, it should be at least admitted that systems analysts and economists were venturing out beyond the gates of academe and applying their theories and tools to real world issues. Although their results were problematic, in doing so, they were paving the way for—perhaps even daring by default—social scientists to join them.

These disciplinary emphases were, like their social sciences predecessors, soon deemphasized. Systems analysis was seen to be brusquely insensitive to public policy issues, especially those of a normative nature.[42] The recognition that economics had its limitations, even in apparently proprietary economic issues,[43] was a major cause for this retrenchment. The agnostic perspective on policy goals, the stress on optimization, the neglect of process and procedure, and the acceptance of microeconomic assumptions regarding human behavior simply proved to be inadequate bases for treating public policy issues.[44] Should, asked Tribe, the Kaldor-Hicks criterion (a variation of Pareto optimality) provide the intellectual grounding for policy applications of cost-benefit analysis and welfare economics in general?[45] The general tendency of these theories and programs to exclude normative considerations—to emphasize efficiency to the exclusion of equity—was unacceptable to political policymakers. Indeed, Dror warned that the economic approach was "fraught with dangers because of the inability to deal adequately with many critical elements of public policy-making and the possible distortion in decision-making resulting therefrom."[46] The shortfalls and outright failures of PPBS to repeat its Defense Department management successes[47] was further and practical evidence to the realization that public policy problems often—perhaps typically—refused to be corrected by textbook solutions because of their very complex, interactive, and changing natures. These growing awarenesses and sensitivities led policy analysts to propose new conceptual paradigms and methodological approaches to what was coming to be known as "squishy" problems.[48]

At the same time, there was a school of positivist-dictated thought which viewed the policy sciences as an opportunity for developing an all-encompassing metatheory of political interactions, whose purpose was to integrate the social and physical sciences—an analog to Einstein's long-sought unifying field theory of physics—as a means of alleviating society ills. Merton asserted that "a major function of applied research is to provide occasions and pressure for interdisciplinary investigations and for the development of a theoretic system of 'basic social science.' "[49] Dror was even more emphatic: "Policy sciences must integrate knowledge from a variety of branches of knowledge into a *supradiscipline* focusing on public policy-making."[50] Although well-intended, these efforts were quickly—and quietly—abandoned for at least three reasons. The emerging discipline lacked the theoretical foundations and empirical substance to support such an enterprise, as Lasswell clearly suggested in "The Policy Orientation" and Merton implied when he set out his research agenda. Furthermore, the definitional debates that would have disruptively ensued and marked progress towards this goal would have been counterproductive to the development of the nascent field as it struggled to achieve a consensual set of foci. Again, the Lasswells and Mertons were careful not to force the policy sciences goals and components into premature intellectual and definitional straitjackets which a metatheory would have entailed. And, finally, an emphasis on metatheory at this early stage would have deflected the policy sciences from other central characteristics, such as their attention and applications to real world social and political dilemmas, and reinforced what critics were already identifying as the approach's drawbacks (e.g., lack of quantitative rigor).

Other scholars, perhaps more modestly, looked to the emerging movement as a means to integrate or at least coordinate several of the social sciences, although with each discipline still retaining its individual identity.[51] Case studies, perhaps based on the Harvard Business School model, were the principal vehicle to this end. The leading text in the field, written with chapters drawn from the various contributing disciplines and case materials, reflects this orientation.[52] Explicit in this theme was the hesitant recognition but still unproven hypothesis that the various disciplines would provide different but hopefully complementary perspectives on a given problem. This movement also waned, largely because it lacked a guiding set of principles. The mere promise of an integrated applied social science emerging as the coherent policy sciences was not sufficient, for it failed to answer the central questions: integrated by what means and to what purpose?

The perceived shortcomings of law, political science, operations research, sociology, economics, psychology, and the other social sciences as they applied to public policy issues led to a general identity crisis and widespread pessimism; Rein and White were not alone when they voiced the concern in "Can Policy Research Help Policy?"[53] Weiss talked in incremental terms about "knowledge creep" and asked if the social sciences could do little more for public policymakers than fulfill an "enlightenment function."[54] Lindblom and Cohen were even more cynical; they claimed that the likelihood of success for policy analysis (or what they termed "professional social inquiry") alleviating policy problems was little better than a random occurrence.[55] These perceptions led, not unexpectedly in the development of a discipline, to what Bozeman calls a crisis in credibility.[56]

These very sobering assessments surely gave legitimate cause to pause: perhaps social complexities were too great to be analytically captured, even by a multidisciplinary net which, by itself, might be too unwieldy to handle. However, as the individual disciplinary wells proved arid, the demand for their curative waters only increased. Still, the disciplines appeared to impose new barriers on the trade of knowledge between them; where information was exchanged (e.g., public choice economics), it often seemed trivial. Alice Rivlin, in her presidential address to the American Economics Association, lamented, "If a golden age of economists' self-confidence ever occurred, it is long since past," and went on to explain how economists can better repackage their special wares to the policymaker's weal, as opposed to rethinking their concepts.[57] The Policy Studies Organization is avowedly directed towards the political science aspects of policy studies, as can be seen in its journals' articles. The Association for Public Policy and Management (and its journal) is heavily economic in its orientation.[58] The policy journals are replete with articles referring to the unique disciplinary contributions of the various fields to policy and, conversely, savaging the blind spots of other disciplines.[59] But the fact that operations research texts now include chapters on policy implementation alongside of their technical exegeses[60] and clinical psychologists are leaders in policy evaluation (e.g., Donald Campbell)[61] is evidence of the general acceptance of the limitations of single discipline policy research (except on very restricted and often technical issues) and the necessity of multidisciplinary policy research.

This is not to suggest that the matter is settled. In place of the strictly unitary disciplinary approach, these experiences have resulted in a return to first principles, to a much more thoroughgoing commitment to multidisciplinary research. This commitment would appear to be more profound and deep-seated than the earlier advocacies for three reasons. First, the initial call for multidisciplinary policy research was relatively isolated, more cant than capability, and—at heart—more threatening to the disciplines' respective identities. Its proponents were few and its opponents were many. Few analysts knew how to engage in multidisciplinary research, for their entire scholastic training was in a single discipline; the Lasswells of the world (and even his disciples) were rare. Lacking the requisite skills, their inclinations and enthusiasms for policy research were understandably reserved. While the contemporary pool might not be particularly well stocked, it is undoubtedly better supplied today than it was twenty years ago. The multidisciplinary training featured in the better university public policy curricula serves to reinforce the establishment of such research approaches. Second, as Heclo pointed out, policy scholars are "seeking to become more truthful to the complexity of events,"[62] a posture which impresses a multidisciplinary set of perspectives on a given social problem for the simple reason that policy issues rarely limit themselves to a single academic discipline. This observation is as pertinent now as it was in Merriam's 1925 APSA address or Merton's 1949 research agenda. Referencing Lasswell, economist Herbert Simon reminded an audience of political scientists that basic cognitive assumptions regarding "rationality" need to be reformulated and integrated into the policy sciences.[63] Finally, there are now a wealth of organizations which specialize in public policy research. These can be found within and without government circles and service both public and private clients. The relative quality of their product, their distinguishing activities, and their institutional half-lives are unquestionably varied, but these criteria are not at issue here. To the point, multidisciplinary, applied policy research no longer has to rely on the fractious and often inhospitable university setting for its institutional bases. For these reasons, it would seem that the multidisciplinary plank of the policy sciences platform rests securely, if not necessarily concretely.

Problem-Oriented and Contextual in Nature

The initial definition of the policy sciences emphasized the policy process and, in particular, knowledge *of* and *in* the policy process.[64] In addition, the policy sciences were explicitly problem-oriented and utilized broad contextual approaches in realization of the perceptions that most social problems could not be incisively extracted and isolated from their political, economic, social, and cultural environments. These two emphases have remained relatively constant and have had a pivotal influence in the development of an approach to policy research. Operationally, they have led to the formulation of a model of the policy process. Lasswell set out an early version of the policy process when he talked about the policy phases: intelligence, promotion, prescription, invocation, application, termination, and appraisal.[65] May and Wildavsky described a policy cycle in which they include agenda setting, issue analysis, implementation, evaluation, and termination.[66] Brewer and deLeon based their understanding of policy analysis on a series of stages upon which they define the policy process: initiation, estimation, selection, implementation, evaluation, and termination.[67] None of these models is universally subscribed to, but its general thrust, form, and acceptance are widely evidenced by the body of public policy literatures which can easily be categorized under one of these headings (evaluation, selection, implementation, etc.).

Two observations are salient here. First, this approach to the policy sciences via the route of the policy process is less topically and more conceptually oriented than some issue-oriented scholars such as housing economists or education evaluators might prefer. The policy analyst is equally concerned with the *process* and the specific issue area at hand. At the same time, this more circumspect approach defers the positing of a generalized theory of social interaction. The first objection does not, of course, imply that specific issues are neglected, for that would stand in rude violation of the problem-oriented tenet of the policy sciences. Nor that barefoot empiricism is irrelevant or otiose for theory building; as Hargrove comments, "Policy analysis that lacks theoretical underpinning is incomplete. Theory that is not tested through application remains academic."[68] After all, Lasswell did talk of knowledge *of* and knowledge *in* the policy process and say that the policy sciences orientation was in part directed towards understanding and educating the policy process. But this emphasis does suggest a broader, more contextual approach to a problem than if one were tightly affixed to a rigidly circumscribed policy issue. Second, these paradigms help the policy sciences discipline move from a purely academic orientation to a more judgmental art and craft. The idea of distinct and identifiable phases in the policy cycle implies that there are approaches, concepts, and methodologies which are more appropriate and applicable to one phase than to another. For instance, cost-benefit analysis is more apropos for policy estimation tasks than it would be for implementation, just as legal skills are more germane to selection than evaluation debates.

Naturally none of these distinctions is immutable, cast in nine yards of typological concrete. Nor should they be. The stages seep into and inform one another; to isolate them would be unrealistic and harmful. Policy formation and selection (what political scientists call decisionmaking) should not be arbitrarily separated; similarly, implementation and evaluation are intimately related.[69] But they can be used as desiderata for organizing and illustrating the following exposition of the evolution of the policy sciences in units of the policy process and its problem-oriented, contextual nature. More to the point for the present discussion, one can observe how for given periods these stages received particular—indeed, undue—emphasis, almost to the point of being shibboleths. Taken in aggregate, across a large number of issue areas, these respective foci have been key determinants in the development of the field. The case can be made for several different subject areas, such as energy policy, civil rights, environmental concerns, national security, and social welfare programs. For purposes of illustration, this discussion will principally allude to examples drawn from American poverty programs, but with great confidence that similar observations and trends can be discerned and replicated in other subject and issue areas, such as the development of new technologies.

By the late 1950s, the inescapable fact that an intolerable number of Americans suffered from various forms of systemic and pervasive poverty—a condition abetted and heightened by racial discrimination—finally moved national policymakers to corrective political actions. Presidents Kennedy and Johnson declared a War on Poverty and committed the considerable resources of the federal government to the fray. One could hardly imagine a more clear-cut case of policy initiation or what some call policy formation: textbook examples of problem recognition, normative imperatives, and policy innovations encompassing a wide variety of options were the marching orders of the day. The policy analysis community was professionally consumed with the charter of devising new programs to alleviate problems identified in health care, urban renewal, housing, education, legal assistance, social welfare, and hunger. Many of these efforts culminated in the Economic Opportunity Act of 1964 and the establishment of the Office of Economic Opportunity (OEO).[70] The emphasis was on quick action rather than contemplative analysis; little attention was paid to requirements of the estimation and evaluation phases—i.e., what might be the forecast effects of these programs on both the specific problems and the surrounding social environments? And how could policymakers tell if the programs were meeting their objectives? Policy and program decisions were made with scant recognition of the complex contextuality of the problems, let alone the proposed solutions. None questioned that the policies would work, that cognizant social engineering was all that was necessary to remedy the now-recognized ills. If America could put a man on the moon its intellectual hubris certainly implied that it could solve the earthly problems of the ghetto.[71] For instance, few argued against increasing welfare payments under the Aid to Families with Dependent Children (AFDC) program, but even fewer considered the effect these transfer payments would have on the family structure and unemployment. Or how the Community Action Programs would warp the political landscapes. Or how urban renewal projects would displace the poor inner city dwellers. However one assesses the outcome of the War on Poverty programs (still an open debate), it is safe to say that the overwhelming focus of policy scientists during this period was on problem recognition and program formulation. This condition influenced the field as a whole, for it virtually excluded consideration of the other phases of the policy process, thereby rendering the best of intentions almost worthless in terms of positive programmatic results.

By the late 1960s, it was clear that most of the OEO's War on Poverty had simply failed or, more generously, had not succeeded. This was repeatedly demonstrated by a series of program evaluations. Head Start, urban New Towns–In Town, and ADFC failures were only indicative of the overall malaise; the number of persons below the poverty level was just as great as it had been a decade before. Apologists argued—not without some justification—that absolute levels of poverty and deprivation were reduced, that the problem was more one of rising expectations than diminished levels of service,[72] and that without these programs the social ills would have escalated into genuine crises in light of the sharply mounting strains and demands on the system.[73] Whatever their actual results, the War on Poverty programs generated a multitude of evaluation studies to address the legitimate question of which programs seemed to be successful and which seemed to fail. The obvious purpose was to learn from these programs so that the social objectives expressed in the early 1960s could be met with new and more effective programs.[74] In many circles, evaluation was considered to be the policy research *sine qua non*, where the analytic pedal hit the policy metal.

The evaluation community was seemingly well prepared for this opportunity. Rossi and Freeman comment that "in the modern era, commitment to the systematic evaluation of programs in such fields as education and public health can be traced to efforts at the turn of the century to provide literacy and occupational training by the most effective and economical means, and to reduce mortality and morbidity from infectious diseases."[75] Daniels and Wirth identify two stages in evaluation research prior to efforts in the mid 1960s, "evaluation research as efficiency" (1910 to

World War II) and "evaluation as field research" (World War II to 1963); their third stage, "evaluation as social experimentation" (1963 to 1974), encompasses this period.[76] Public health scholars, such as Suchman, were central in the development of program evaluation and evaluation research and, in particular, in urging the application of evaluation skills to policy programs rather than academic exercises.[77]

Now, virtually en masse, the policy research community focused almost exclusively on policy evaluation. The evaluation phase of the policy cycle certainly benefited from this concentration of attention. New methodologies, often from social and clinical psychology, were brought to bear while others were adjusted to fit special needs. Federal government and private foundation (e.g., the Russell Sage Foundation) fundings were extensive. Problem-oriented evaluation research stood poised to make substantial contributions to public policymaking.

The embarrassment of resource and methodological riches had one serious drawback which was to prove all but fatal. Most of these evaluators clamoring at the policy research banks had spent their entire professional experience within academic circles and had developed little appreciation for the policy sensitivities necessary in working with public officials or making sure that their findings and recommendations matched the clients' needs. The possibility of institutional hostility had not occurred to them, even though it surely affected research designs and evaluation procedures. Academic purposes and bureaucratic objectives presented very different dance cards. Many evaluators did not recognize these differences or, if they did, were reluctant to learn the new steps.

Unfortunately, like program initiation, evaluation proved a questionable activity. Not only were the evaluators seldom able to identify the sources of programmatic shortcomings, but they were rarely able to be responsive to the policymakers' needs for better information. Evaluation *qua* policy analysis received a poor reputation from the very sponsors who were financially supporting it. "Relevance" versus "rigor" controversies undercut numerous evaluations. Most critically, they were not able to address the pivotal policy questions: Are these programs "working"? If not, why not, and what can be done? Regardless, for whatever reasons and to whatever outcomes, the policy research community during the late 1960s and early 1970s was fixated on questions of policy evaluation to the deprivation of the other stages.

Given these evaluation shortcomings, it is not surprising that in the mid 1970s, the focus again switched as policy researchers believed that they had identified the root cause of program failure. One report commented:

> We became increasingly bothered in the late 1960s by those aspects of the exercise of government authority bound up with implementation. Results achieved by the programs of that decade were widely recognized as inadequate. One clear source of failure emerged: political and bureaucratic aspects of the implementation process were, in great measure, left outside both the considerations of participants of government and the calculations of formal policy analysts who assisted them.[78]

No one should doubt that in the early 1970s implementation, the waltz of the bureaucrats, was a neglected phase—both conceptually and operationally—in the policy process, a sorry commentary on the inability of public administration to make itself relevant. Pressman and Wildavsky, in preparation for their landmark study, found virtually no antecedent research on implementation issues.[79] It was professionally reassuring for policy researchers to suspect that the programs themselves, as conceived, were equal to the task and that the real culprit of policy failure was the delivery system, not the concept. Claiming that implementation was the "missing link" separating program formation and program success, the policy research community moved enthusiastically to the study of this phase of the policy process.[80] Berman and McLaughlin discussed implementation in the context of federally sponsored education programs while Derthick explained the founderings of the New Towns–In Town urban renewal programs as multiple failures in implementation politics. The nexus between the federal and local governments was seen as especially guilty of implementation crimes. Recognizing the dilemmas presented by policy implementation, Williams proposed "implementation analysis" as a means of including implementation strategies in an analysis before decisions would have to be reached;[81] implementation analysis would thus be part of the estimation and selection phases of the policy process. This would be one way of ensuring that the policymaker appreciated the problems that faulty or slipshod implementation could engender and, armed with such knowledge, execute effective policies and programs.

Like the earlier emphases on program initiation and evaluation, this focus on implementation was undoubtedly salutary. Great amounts of case study material were developed and brought to bear, highlighting the difficulties of policy implementation and how they might be foreseen and reduced. Policy scholars offered implementation typologies[82] while a few proposed tentative first steps towards a general theory of policy implementation.[83] And, again, like the earlier problems with initiation and evaluation, this emphasis on implementation produced more confusion than clarification. Implementation turned out to be far more complex and difficult than the implementation analysis proponents had suspected.[84] Regardless of the outcome of these efforts, one can safely say that the policy research community during the mid to late 1970s heavily attended questions of policy implementation to the relative exclusion of the other phases of the policy process.

Towards the end of the 1970s, governments on all levels were besieged with demands for greater economy, demands reinforced by reduced revenues as taxpayers insisted on less waste and greater economy in government. California's Proposition 13— which rolled back property taxes, hence local government revenues—was indicative; social welfare programs, suspect during the best of times, came under particular scrutiny.[85] This tendency was further supported by the political inclinations of elected representatives who were ideologically opposed to "big government."[86] In light of these developments, program termination—under such labels as cutback management, sunset legislation, and fiscal retrenchment—became a prevalent theme in policy research, although not to the extent of the previous emphases on program implementation and evaluation. Examples from the War on Poverty are easy to identify. Under the Nixon administration, Howard Phillips was explicitly chartered to eliminate the OEO, even while he was its director. Although the Community Services Act of 1974 officially ended the OEO's existence, many of its programs continued into the 1980s when they began to succumb to the reduction onslaughts of the Reagan administration's budget cuts. The financial tribulations of New York City, only one of several financially endangered cities, gave additional credence to and cause for termination studies and proposed tactics.[87]

With bountiful materials and ready clients at their disposal, policy scientists turned their attention to describing and prescribing termination strategies, especially on the embattled municipal fronts. Alas, like the other emphases on the different phases of the policy process, termination studies proved similarly unable to provide solid programmatic advice. For a variety of reasons, most of the programs and institutions ticketed for elimination proved remarkably resistant to the policy termination axe, thereby offering additional evidence for an affirmative answer to Kaufman's question: Are government organizations immortal?[88] Another policy research trend had come and gone without leaving much in the way of positive, worthwhile recommendations.

Certainly none of these concentrations represented wasted efforts. Immense literatures have been written, disseminated, and perhaps taken to heart. No doubt the policy communities—both analysts and policymakers—are much wiser than they were twenty years ago. Much has been learned about each of these areas and their unique characteristics. But what has been largely overlooked from a conceptual vantage point is the need for integration and balance, the initial Lasswell injunction that these are not discretely separable stages. This was a necessary lesson, although an expensive one in terms of the costs incurred by deficient programs and dashed expectations. Each of the policy stages is by necessity closely tied to the others, as the War on Poverty vividly illustrates. The policy process operates as a series of iterative stages and feedback loops: initiation is tied to estimation; selection must be advised by implementation, just as evaluation must precede and inform termination.[89] I have written elsewhere that initiation and termination—the beginning and the end of the policy cycle—are cut from the same conceptual and analytic bolts.[90] There is a growing acceptance that the policy process is a seamless web rather than a disjointed series of individual stages or phases. If the policy sciences are to retain their problem orientation, they will require a variety of contextual and methodological perspectives to encompass the full ramifications of knowledge in and of the policy process. Thus, we can see how the evolution of the problem-oriented, contextual nature of the policy sciences has come full circle back to some of the integrating hypotheses set out by such as Merton and Lasswell.

Irrespective of the clarity or cogency of these founding visions, however, the reality is that the policy sciences, perhaps more than any other intellectual pursuit, are affected by events external to and beyond their manipulation. Methodological sophistications and narrow foci cannot escape this charge. Moreover, the policy sciences are, by definition, problem-oriented, so they cannot absent themselves from the political and social environments without abandoning an integral part of their vitality and literal *raison d'être*. While this is not an ironclad dictum—they clearly should not run higgledy-piggledy after every issue of topicality—it is evident that they have been profoundly affected by their heritage of problem orientation, even if it means surrendering to conditions largely beyond their control. There is no ready solution for this pell-mell situation, although some promising amelioratives, such as Lasswell's developmental construct, have been proposed. The reason is clear: the policy sciences have deliberately set themselves in the midst of the real world maelstrom and must therefore endure whatever political tides and eddies might swirl their way. The discipline's professional challenge, then, is to be able to accommodate and even prosper in the face of these buffets without being unduly warped. In terms of the problem-oriented, contextual nature of the approach, this requires a balanced, coordinated view of the policy process, one less dictated by narrow foci on easy aspects, however convenient and comfortable such perspectives might be.

Explicitly Normative in Perspective

The policy sciences, almost from their very conception, have been explicitly normative in their content and concern with human values. In Lasswell's words, "The policy sciences approach . . . calls forth a very considerable clarification of the value goals involved in policy," towards what he called the "policy sciences of democracy."[91] Lasswell and Kaplan defined the policy sciences as providing "intelligence pertinent to the integration of values realized by and embodied in interpersonal relations," which "prizes not the glory of a depersonalized state or the efficiency of a social mechanism, but human dignity and the realization of human capacities."[92] This emphasis on values—especially those relating to the protection and advancement of human dignity—has remained a constant touchstone of the policy sciences approach. Equally important is the idea that these values can be recognized and made an explicit part of the analysis of social issues.[93] The imperative rings true, even if the means to this end are much in doubt and dispute.[94] Can anybody, the policy scientist would ask, understand civil rights policies, welfare transfer payments, or comparative worth legislation without a clear acknowledgment that all persons *ought* to have equal access without bias attributable to race, creed, sex, or religion? The abortion and surrogate parent debates are unintelligible without an appreciation and inclusion of moral positions.

In spite of these early strictures, the normative aspects of the policy sciences were neglected by virtually all its proponents. Three reasons might be suggested for this condition. First, some claimed that governments and programs do little more than "muddle through" and insisted that an incremental approach to policy would encompass or balance any normative postures that might occur. These might "appear" at a sub rosa, undebated level, but, nevertheless, they would be de facto incorporated, thus relieving the analyst of any normative responsibilities.[95] Second, others argued that quantitative methodologies, such as practiced in operations research and economics, were essentially value-free and therefore did not have to concern themselves with questions of ethics or values. An unspoken reliance on Dewey's rationality, the fidelity of the Weberian bureaucracy, and positivism in general underlaid this assumption. And, third, a sizable number of policy analysts argued that values were the exclusive domain of the policymaker, that for analysts to intrude on that realm, to interject their values, would be unwarranted (i.e., beyond their professional competencies, expertise, and charter) and perhaps even "wrong" in the sense of the democratic ethic.[96]

Of course none of these arguments is without some merit, but they clearly deviate fom the original enunciations of the policy sciences. Even more cogently, the refusal to consider explicitly the normative and ideological aspects of the policy process has repeatedly, almost insistently, resulted in empty analyses which inadequately "explained" what had happened or what might be for three reasons. In the first place, a value-free approach might be sufficient for a very limited systems analysis problem such as the feasibility of alternative mass transit systems, but even this assumption is questionable because it does not consider who is served (and why) by the transit system. What is beyond dispute is that the broad, societally relevant contextual issues addressed by the policy sciences simply cannot be understood without the open recognition of pertaining social values. To treat them on an incremental basis fundamentally finesses the problem by tacitly assuming that "everything will work out all right." Dror effectively demonstrated the bankruptcy of the incrementalist argument as it pertained to values years ago.[97] Simply, values are too central to the various stages of the policy process to permit them to be covertly inserted, neglected, or left to some hidden marginalist hand "muddling through." Second, most observers can agree that the strictly quantitative approach to policy problems is insufficient, that matters of equity must be broached and consciously included. Less at dispute, then, is the goal than the means to that goal.[98] Furthermore, it is now widely conceded that even the choice of methodologies implies a powerful set of normative values and analytic assumptions which will perforce shape the ultimate analysis. The idea of rationality in government and a benignly compliant bureaucracy have been shown to be flatly wrong.[99] In short, there is no such thing as a "value-free" study or even methodology. And, third, few analysts would claim that they can "resolve" normative issues in their analyses, but an increasingly large number will admit that they can make such considerations an open element of their work and ultimate advice. There is now less reason for ignoring the value components of an issue, especially since these criteria have been revealed as being so pivotal in the policy process and actual policymaking.

Examples of normative standards and political ideologies as they apply to and affect policy analysis are readily available. For instance, President Reagan's "New Federalism" is "predicated on the assumption that programs dismantled at the federal level can, if desired, be reconstituted at the state or municipal levels and be more directly attuned to the needs of their constituents. The evidence for this assumption is clearly open to debate."[100] Reagan spokespersons articulated this position in a report prepared by the Department of Housing and Urban Development: "State and local governments have amply demonstrated that, properly unfettered, they will make better decisions than the federal government acting for them."[101] The transition to the "privatization" of formerly public services (e.g., social welfare service and criminal incarceration) is a certain signal of value judgments. Normative overtones and prior persuasions would be hard to overlook in the administration's view of compensatory education programs:

> It's simply something the federal government shouldn't be doing. Education is the province of the states and localities . . . and no matter how effective a federal program may be, it still intrudes on the state and local domains.[102]

The attempted decision to abolish the Department of Energy was no less ideologically pronounced; in the words of DOE's self-authored sunset review document:

> Many of the department's programs are no longer valid within the context of the federal role in the energy sector of the economy. . . . In the view of the demonstrated success of energy markets in those cases where they have been allowed to function freely, and given the limited role and responsibilities of the federal government in this sector of the economy, it is no longer necessary or appropriate to maintain a Cabinet-level Department of Energy. The department was established to address a set of problems that were peculiar to their time and that were largely the result of a philosophy that stressed excessive government intervention in the energy market in the first place.[103]

Similar illustrations from very different issue areas can be found in the debates over national security, in which the litmus test is whether one trusts the "evil empire" of the Soviet Union, and social welfare programs, which key upon the value of the "nuclear" family. The conflict between the public's right to protect its collective self and sanctity of individual privacy—a dilemma most poignantly revisited by the spreading AIDS epidemic—is constantly being played out on the policy proscenium. Environmental debates are similarly couched. These policies, however, "objectively" presented with quantitative indicators such as missile warheads, AFDC recipients, infection rates, or preserved wilderness acres, are directly derived from one's moral and ideological precepts.

One can thus assume that normative standards are increasingly being made a visible part of political decisionmaking. If policy scientists wish to continue the quality of their access and advice, then it is equally clear that values must be openly and candidly included in their policy analyses. The ideas (or hopes) that they could be ignored or subverted to technical constructs or sophistications (as is still assumed by many systems analysts) are no longer tenable, if they ever were. Although policy scientists may not be able to convince the political policymakers of the rectitude of any given set of norms, analysts can at least explicate the contending values and thereby permit policymakers to make an honest, more informed (i.e., less hidden) judgment. Thus, for a third time, the policy sciences have evolved in such a way that they have returned to the third element of the original Lasswellian framework. It might be difficult to predict with any confidence what effect this realization might have or how it will be implemented. It is probable, however, that the normative component of the policy sciences will have a decided influence both conceptually and in the workaday world of the policy sciences.

IN REVIEW

The policy sciences have matured from their modest origins in societally relevant knowledge to what many describe as a "growth industry." They have developed a set of disciplinary implements and applied them with occasional discernment to social and political issues. They have also developed a better understanding of the policy process, that is, how to translate good intentions into good programs. The multidisciplinary, problem-oriented, and normative elements have not always been graciously accepted, but their wisdom and relevance now seem secure. In short, the institutionalization and quality of policy advice has improved because of the intellectual contributions of the various disciplines, especially when taken in unison. These are not trivial achievements.

This is not to suggest that the policy sciences represent a single accepted conceptual model, that all is well, and that there are not grounds for future refinements and improvements. Some techniques previously accepted are now considered questionable on technical, procedural, and normative grounds. For instance, the use of cost-benefit analysis, once an analytic touchstone, has been severely criticized in terms of its operating assumptions (e.g., choice of the discount rate), participants (e.g., questions of standing), and normative underpinnings.[104] Still others loom promising on the methodological horizon (e.g., forensic analysis and risk assessment). Thus, it would be expected to see new analytic modes move into and out of the policy sciences as they prove (or disprove) their worth. Similarly, emerging issue areas (especially those involving the effect of new technologies on society such as in the fields of medicine and genetic engineering) will probably require new perspectives and tools, many of these emanating from the physical and natural sciences. Thus, it can be hopefully predicted that the "supply" or "advice" side of the policy sciences coin will continue to evolve in a "politic, cautious, and meticulous" manner, but always "full of high sentence" to "advise the prince."

ENDNOTES

1. William N. Dunn, *Public Policy Analysis* (Englewood Cliffs, NJ: Prentice-Hall, 1981), pp. 8–9.
2. Barbara Tuchman, *The March of Folly* (New York: Knopf, 1984), chap. 2.
3. The tradition is documented by Herbert Goldhamer, *The Adviser* (New York: Elsevier, 1978).
4. The Temple at Delphi had many of the trappings of a contemporary "think tank." Maidens would render prophecies after undertaking the appropriate ceremonies. However, these were not delivered directly to the "clients" until they had been translated into hexameter by the temple priests, thereby presenting ample opportunity for revision, expansion, and amplification. Considerable care went into preparation of the policy advice that the Oracle ultimately delivered to its suppliants, the best known example being the Delphic prophecy (ambiguous as it might have been) which girded the Athenian resolve against the invading Persian armies of Xerxes at the battle of Salamis (480

B.C.). See Herodotus, *The Histories*, Book VII (Baltimore: Penguin Classics, 1972), pp. 441–525. I am indebted to John E. Koehler for this example.

5. Tuchman, *The March of Folly*, chap. 4, offers an illustration of this relationship in the context of the British monarchy's obstinate efforts to retain England's hold on her American colonies.

6. See Dunn, *Public Policy Analysis*, pp. 12–14.

7. Peter B. Evans, Dietrich Rueschemeyer, and Theda Skocpol, "On the Road Toward a More Adequate Understanding of the State," in Peter B. Evans, Dietrich Rueschemeyer, and Theda Skocpol, eds., *Bringing the State Back In* (Cambridge: Cambridge University Press, 1985), p. 357. Also see Douglas E. Ashford, "Welfare States as Institutional Choices," in Norman Furniss, ed., *Futures for the Welfare State* (Bloomington: Indiana University Press, 1986).

8. The activities of the English reformers Charles Booth, Seebohm Rowntree, and Beatrice and Sidney Webb are covered in Martin Bulmer, *The Uses of Social Research* (London: George Allen & Unwin, 1982), chap. 1; a history of the American Progressive era is Richard Hofstadter, *The Age of Reform* (New York: Vintage Books, 1955).

9. William James, *Pragmatism* (Cambridge, MA: Harvard University Press, 1907), and John Dewey, *The Quest for Certainty* (New York: Putnam, 1929), and *The Public and Its Problems* (London: Allen & Unwin, 1946), are representative of their respective contributions.

10. Typical of Weber's work in this area are his essays "Science and Politics" (part II) and "Bureaucracy" (chap. VII), in H. H. Gerth and C. Wright Mills, eds. and trans., *From Max Weber: Essays in Sociology* (New York: Oxford University Press, 1946).

11. Harold D. Lasswell, "The Policy Orientation," in Daniel Lerner and Harold D. Lasswell, eds., *The Policy Sciences* (Stanford, CA: Stanford University Press, 1951), and Harold D. Lasswell, *A Pre-View of Policy Sciences* (New York: American Elsevier, 1971). The durability of Lasswell's vision is remarkable; see Douglas Torgerson, "Contextual Orientation in Policy Analysis: The Contributions of Harold Lasswell," *Policy Sciences* 18, no. 3 (November 1985): 241–262; and Peter deLeon, "Trends in Policy Sciences Research: Determinants and Developments," *European Journal of Political Research* 14, no. 1 (1986): 3–22.

12. Karl Mannheim, *Ideology and Utopia*; Louis Wirth and Edward Shils, trans. (New York: Harcourt, Brace, 1936), p. 99. It is interesting that Mannheim excluded such thoroughly Germanic disciplines as public administration, economics, and law from his list of contributors.

13. Charles E. Merriam, "Progress in Political Research," *American Political Science Review* 20, no. 1 (February 1926): 1–13; at pp. 8–9.

Barry D. Karl, *Charles E. Merriam and the Study of Politics* (Chicago: University of Chicago Press, 1975), elaborates on Merriam's monumental contributions to the study of politics. It is scarcely coincidence that Lasswell was one of Merriam's students at the University of Chicago.

14. Peter T. Manicas, *A History and Philosophy of the Social Sciences* (New York: Basil Blackwell, 1987), p. 211.

15. Dwight Waldo, *The Study of Public Administration* (New York: Random House, 1955), briefly sets out this progression. It is instructive to note the publication dates of the first two major texts in public administration, Leonard D. White, *Introduction to the Study of Public Administration* (New York: Macmillan, 1926); and F. W. Willoughby, *Principles of Public Administration* (Washington, DC: Brookings Institution, 1927).

16. E.g., Robert K. Merton, "The Unanticipated Consequences of Purposive Social Action." *American Sociological Review* 1, no. 4 (December 1936): 894–904.

17. E.g., Mitchell's 1919 address to the American Statistical Association, reprinted in Wesley C. Mitchell, *The Backward Art of Spending Money and Other Essays* (New York: McGraw-Hill, 1937). Mitchell was instrumental in the creation of the National Bureau of Economic Research and, in 1920, was appointed its first director of research.

18. The creation of the SSRC is detailed by Gene M. Lyons, *The Uneasy Partnership* (New York: Russell Sage Foundation, 1969), chap. 2, "The Shaping of Social Science."

19. Donald T. Critchlow, *The Brookings Institution, 1916–1952: Expertise and the Public Interest in a Democratic Society* (DeKalb: Northern Illinois University Press, 1985); also Lyons, *The Uneasy Partnership*.

20. Other individuals (and disciplines) cited by William Ascher, "The Evolution of the Policy Sciences: Understanding the Rise and Avoiding the Fall," *Journal of Policy Analysis and Management* 5, no. 2 (Winter 1985): 365–373, at p. 366, include Edward Sapir (linguistics); George Herbert Mead, Clyde Kluckhohn, and Margaret Mead (anthropology); Myres McDougal (law); and Harry Stock Sullivan (psychiatry).

21. Robert S. Lynd, *Knowledge for What? The Place of Social Science in the American Culture* (Princeton, NJ: Princeton University Press, 1939), p. 9.

22. A controversy we shall revisit in the next chapter, especially how the NSF deliberations and funding excluded the social sciences; see Lyons, *The Uneasy Partnership*, chap. 5; also Nelson W. Polsby, *Political Innovation in America* (New Haven: Yale University Press, 1984), chap. 2.

23. Richard G. Hewlett and Oscar E. Anderson, Jr., *A History of the*

United States Atomic Energy Commission: The New World, 1939–1946 (University Park: Pennsylvania State University Press, 1962), is the official AEC history; a briefer account is in Polsby, *Political Innovation in America*, chap. 2.

24. Quoted in Lyons, *The Uneasy Partnership*, p. 133. Lyons and Polsby, *Political Innovation in America*, provide accounts, if not good explanations, of this preclusion.

25. Robert K. Merton, "The Role of Applied Social Science in the Formation of Policy: A Research Memorandum," *Philosophy of Science* 16, no. 3 (July 1949): 161–181; quotations at pp. 167, 163, 170, 169–170, and 171, respectively. Emphasis in original.

26. Lasswell, "The Policy Orientation," pp. 3, 4, 8, and 14, respectively.

27. Perhaps the best example is his 1956 presidential address delivered to the American Political Science Association meeting; Harold D. Lasswell, "The Political Science of Science," *American Political Science Review* 50, no. 4 (December 1956): 961–979.

28. See, *inter alia*, Harold D. Lasswell, *Psychopathology and Politics* (Chicago: University of Chicago Press, 1930); *World Politics and Personal Insecurity* (New York: Free Press, 1935); and "What Psychiatrists and Political Scientists Can Learn from One Another," *Psychiatry* 1 (1938): 33–39.

29. Torgerson, "Contextual Orientation in Policy Analysis," p. 245.

30. Harold D. Lasswell, "Legal Education and Public Policy: Professional Training in the Public Interest," in Harold D. Lasswell, *The Analysis of Political Behavior* (London: Routledge & Kegan Paul, 1947).

31. Lasswell, "The Policy Orientation," p. 11; also see Torgerson, "Contextual Orientation in Policy Analysis," pp. 247–248.

32. Harold D. Lasswell and Abraham Kaplan, *Power and Society* (New Haven: Yale University Press, 1950); and Harold D. Lasswell, *A Pre-View of Policy Sciences* (New York: American Elsevier, 1971).

33. E.g., Harold D. Lasswell et al., *Language of Politics: Studies in Quantitative Semantics* (New York: George Stewart, 1949).

34. A 1976 *festschrift* honoring Lasswell is illustrative; Dwaine Marvick, ed., *Harold D. Lasswell on Political Sociology* (Chicago: University of Chicago Press, 1977). Also see the collection of essays assembled by Lerner and Lasswell, eds., *The Policy Sciences*.

35. E.g., Paul Kecskemeti, "The 'Policy Sciences': Aspiration and Outlook," *World Politics* 5, no. 4 (July 1952): 520–535.

36. Robert L. Lineberry, "Policy Analysis, Policy Sciences, and Political Science," paper presented at the American Political Science Association meeting, Chicago, 1982; also Ascher, "The Evolution of the Policy Sciences." The theme is detailed at length by David M. Ricci, *The Tragedy of Political Science: Politics,*

Scholarship, and Democracy (New Haven: Yale University Press, 1984).

37. Personal conversation, 1976. Robert K. Merton related a similar uncertainty as to the causes for this lapse (personal conversation, 1987).

38. Lineberry, "Policy Analysis, Policy Sciences, and Political Science," p. 7.

39. Giandomenico Majone and Edward S. Quade, "Introduction," in Giandomenico Majone and Edward S. Quade, eds., *Pitfalls of Analysis* (New York: Wiley, 1980), p. 5. The same assumption appears seven years later in Hugh J. Miser and Edward S. Quade, eds., *Handbook of Systems Analysis: Craft Issues and Procedural Choices* (New York: Elsevier, 1987).

40. Charles J. Hitch and Roland N. McKean, *The Economics of Defense in the Nuclear Age* (Cambridge, MA: Harvard University Press, 1960), explain and illustrate these procedures; their applications in Robert McNamara's Defense Department were later documented by Alain Enthoven and C. Wayne Smith, *How Much Is Enough?* (New York: Harper & Row, 1970).

41. Edward S. Quade and William I. Boucher, eds., *Systems Analysis and Policy Planning* (New York: Elsevier, 1968).

42. Ida Hoos, *Systems Analysis in Public Policy* (Berkeley: University of California Press, 1972).

43. As noted both professionally, Walter W. Heller, "What's Right with Economics," *American Economics Review* 65, no. 1 (March 1975): 1–26, who, in his AEA presidential address, warned that the "chorus of self-criticism has risen to a new crescendo" (at p. 1); and popularly, Wade Green, "Economists in Recession: After an Inflation of Errors and a Depletion of Theory," *New York Times Magazine,* May 12, 1972, pp. 18–19, 56–58.

44. Lawrence M. Mead, "The Interactive Problem in Policy Analysis," *Policy Sciences* 16, no. 1 (September 1983): 45–66; and Susan B. Hanson, "Public Policy Analysis: Some Recent Developments and Current Problems," *Policy Studies Journal* 12, no. 1 (September 1983): 14–42.

45. Laurence H. Tribe, "Policy Analysis: Analysis or Ideology?" *Philosophy & Public Policy* 2, no. 1 (Fall 1972): 71. Tribe characterized the reliance on microeconomic assumptions as "through a slide rule darkly."

46. Yehezkel Dror, "Policy Analysts: A New Professional Role in Government Service," *Public Administration Review* 27, no. 3 (September 1967): 198. Reprinted in Yehezkel Dror, *Ventures in Policy Analysis* (New York: American Elsevier, 1971), chap. 21.

47. See Aaron Wildavsky, *The Politics of the Budgetary Process* (Boston: Little, Brown, 1979), chap. 6.

48. Ralph E. Strauch, " 'Squishy' Problems and Quantitative

Methods," *Policy Sciences* 6, no. 2 (June 1975): 175–184; and Ralph E. Strauch, "A Critical Look at Quantitative Methodology," *Policy Analysis* 2, no. 1 (Winter 1976): 121–144.
49. Merton, "The Role of Applied Social Sciences in the Formation of Policy," p. 171.
50. Yehezkel Dror, "Prolegomena to Policy Sciences," *Policy Sciences* 1, no. 1 (Spring 1970): 138; emphasis added. This theme is elaborated in Yehezkel Dror, *Design for the Policy Sciences* (New York: American Elsevier, 1971).
51. See James C. Charlesworth, ed., *Integration of the Social Sciences Through Policy Analysis* (Philadelphia: American Academy of Political and Social Sciences, Monograph no. 14, 1972); and James C. Coleman, *Policy Research in the Social Sciences* (Morristown, NJ: General Learning Press, 1972).
52. Raymond A. Bauer and Kenneth J. Gergen, eds., *The Study of Policy Formation* (New York: Free Press, 1968).
53. Martin Rein and Sheldon H. White, "Can Policy Research Help Policy?" *Public Interest*, no. 49 (Fall 1979): 119–136.
54. Carol H. Weiss, ed., *Using Social Science in Public Policy Making* (Lexington, MA: Heath, 1977).
55. Charles E. Lindblom and David K. Cohen, *Usable Knowledge* (New Haven: Yale University Press, 1979).
56. Barry Bozeman, "The Credibility of Policy Analysis: Between Method and Use," *Policy Studies Journal* 14, no. 4 (June 1986): 519–539; and David Landsbergen and Barry Bozeman, "Credibility Logic and Policy Analysis," *Knowledge* 8, no. 4 (June 1987): 625–648.
57. Alice M. Rivlin, "Economics and the Political Process," *American Economics Review* 77, no. 1 (March 1987): 1–10, at p. 1. Rivlin is extremely knowledgeable in both facets of her address, having been the first director of the Congressional Budget Office. Also William A. Niskanen, "Economics and Politicians," *Journal of Public Policy and Management* 5, no. 2 (Winter 1986): 234–244; Niskanen served four years on the Council of Economic Advisors.
58. E.g., the papers assembled from the association's 1981 meetings were almost entirely based upon microeconomics; see Richard J. Zeckhauser and Derek Leebaert, eds., *What Role for Government?* (Durham, NC: Duke University Press, 1983).
59. E.g., David J. Webber, "Analyzing Political Feasibility: Political Scientists' Unique Contribution to Policy Analysis," *Policy Studies Journal* 14, no. 4 (June 1986): 545–554; Richard I. Hofferbert, "Policy Evaluation, Democratic Theory, and the Division of Scholarly Labor," *Policy Studies Review* 5, no. 3 (February 1986): 511–519; and Paul C. Stern, "What Economics Doesn't Say About Energy Use," *Journal of Policy Analysis and Management* 5,

no. 2 (Winter 1986): 200–227. Compare Hofferbert with Anne L. Schneider, "Evaluation Research and Political Science: An Argument Against the Scholarly Division of Labor," *Policy Studies Review* 6, no. 2 (November 1986): 222–232.
60. E.g., Richard C. Larson and Amedeo Odoni, *Urban Operations Research* (Englewood Cliffs, NJ: Prentice-Hall, 1981).
61. Donald T. Campbell, "Reforms as Experiments," *American Psychologist* 24, no. 4 (April 1969): 409–429; and Donald T. Campbell and J. C. Stanley, *Experimental and Quasi-Experimental Designs for Research* (Skokie, IL: Rand McNally, 1966). The Policy Studies Organization Award for exemplary methodological contribution to policy studies is named after Campbell.
62. H. Hugh Heclo, "Review Article: Policy Analysis," *British Journal of Politics* 2, no. 2 (1972): 87.
63. Herbert A. Simon, "Human Nature in Politics: The Dialogue of Psychology with Political Science," *American Political Science Review* 79, no. 2 (June 1985): 293–304; more specific examples are found in Daniel Kahneman, Paul Slovic, and Amos Tversky, eds., *Judgment Under Uncertainty: Heuristics and Biases* (New York: Cambridge University Press, 1982).
64. Harold D. Lasswell, "The Emerging Conception of the Policy Sciences," *Policy Sciences* 1, no. 1 (Spring 1970): 3.
65. Harold D. Lasswell, *The Decision Process* (College Park: University of Maryland Press, 1956); also Lasswell, *A Pre-View of Policy Sciences*.
66. Judith May and Aaron Wildavsky, eds., *The Policy Cycle* (Beverly Hills, CA: Sage, 1978).
67. Garry D. Brewer and Peter deLeon, *The Foundations of Policy Analysis* (Homewood, IL: Dorsey Press, 1983).
68. Edwin C. Hargrove, "The Search for Implementation Theory," in Zeckhauser and Leebaert, eds., *What Role for Government?* p. 280.
69. A point made by Angela Browne and Aaron Wildavsky, "What Should Evaluation Mean to Implementation?" and "Implementation as Mutual Adaptation," in Jeffrey L. Pressman and Aaron Wildavsky, *Implementation . . .* (Berkeley: University of California Press, 1984 ed.), chaps. 9 and 10, respectively. This theme is highlighted throughout their text by Brewer and deLeon, *The Foundations of Policy Analysis*.
70. These activities will be discussed in greater detail in the following chapter's account of the War on Poverty; Robert A. Levine, *The Poor Ye Need Not Have with You: Lessons from the War on Poverty* (Cambridge, MA; MIT Press, 1970), describes the 1964–1969 period from the perspective of a member of the OEO.
71. The metaphor was given currency and debunked by Richard N. Nelson, *The Moon and the Ghetto* (New York: Norton, 1977).

72. A possibility well argued by Aaron Wildavsky, *Speaking Truth to Power* (Boston: Little, Brown, 1979), chap. 4.
73. John E. Schwarz, *America's Hidden Success: A Reassessment of Twenty Years of Public Policy* (New York: Norton, 1983).
74. See the two volumes by Eleanor Clelimsky, ed., *A Symposium on the Uses of Evaluation by Federal Agencies* (McLean, VA: MITRE Corporation, 1977).
75. Peter H. Rossi and Howard E. Freeman, *Evaluation: A Systematic Approach* (Beverly Hills, CA: Sage, 1985), pp. 20–29, provide a brief history of evaluation; quotation on p. 21.
76. M. Daniels and C. J. Wirth, "Paradigms of Evaluation Research: The Development of an Important Policymaking Component," *American Review of Public Administration* 17, no. 1 (Spring 1983): 33–45.
77. Edward A. Suchman, *Evaluation Research* (New York: Russell Sage Foundation, 1967), makes this distinction; also see Francis G. Caro, ed., *Readings in Evaluation Research* (New York: Russell Sage Foundation, 1969).
78. Research Seminar on Bureaucracy, Politics, and Policy, *A Report on Studies of Implementation in the Public Sector* (Cambridge, MA: John F. Kennedy School of Government, Harvard University, 1973).
79. Pressman and Wildavsky, *Implementation*, 1973 ed., app. A.
80. Edwin C. Hargrove, *The Missing Link: The Study of Implementation* (Washington, DC: Urban Institute, 1975). Also see Daniel A. Mazmanian and Paul A. Sabatier, eds., *Effective Implementation Policy* (Lexington, MA: Heath, 1981) and *Implementation and Public Policy* (Glencoe, IL: Scott Foresman, 1983), for overviews of what has become a vast literature.
81. Walter Williams, "Implementation Analysis and Assessment," *Policy Analysis* 1, no. 3 (Summer 1975): 531–566. Also Charles Wolf, Jr., "A Theory for Nonmarket Failure: Framework for Implementation Analysis," *Journal of Law and Economics* 22, no. 1 (April 1979): 107–139.
82. Eugene C. Bardach, *The Implementation Game* (Cambridge, MA: MIT Press, 1977).
83. Hargrove, "The Search for Implementation Theory." Also Paul Sabatier, "Top-Down and Bottom-Up Models of Policy Implementation: A Critical Analysis and Suggested Synthesis," *Journal of Public Policy* 6, no. 1 (June 1986): 21–48.
84. Two critiques of implementation research are Bjorn Wittrock and Peter deLeon, "Policy as a Moving Target: A Call for Conceptual Realism," *Policy Studies Review* 6, no. 1 (August 1986): 44–60; and Stephen H. Linder and B. Guy Peters, "A Design Perspective on Policy Implementation: The Fallacies of Misplaced Prescription," *Policy Studies Review* 6, no. 3 (February

1987): 459–475. Also see the 1984 edition of Pressman and Wildavsky, *Implementation*.
85. A seminal series of articles was assembled by Eugene C. Bardach for *Policy Sciences* 7, no. 2 (June 1976), a special issue devoted to policy termination.
86. Peter deLeon, "A Theory of Policy Termination," and James M. Cameron, "Ideology and Policy Termination," in May and Wildavsky, eds., *The Policy Cycle*, chaps. 12 and 13, respectively.
87. Charles H. Levine et al., *The Politics of Retrenchment* (Beverly Hills, CA: Sage, 1981); Demetrios Caralay, *Doing More with Less* (New York: Graduate Program in Public Policy, Columbia University, 1982); and Peter deLeon, "Policy Evaluation and Program Termination," *Policy Studies Review* 2, no. 4 (May 1983): 631–647.
88. Herbert Kaufman, *Are Government Organizations Immortal?* (Washington, DC: Brookings Institution, 1976).
89. Some policy researchers have recognized this; see, for example, Mead, "The Interactive Problem in Policy Analysis"; deLeon, "Policy Evaluation and Program Termination"; Browne and Wildavsky, "What Should Evaluation Mean to Implementation"; and Linder and Peters, "A Design Perspective on Policy Implementation."
90. Peter deLeon, "Public Policy Termination: An End and a Beginning," *Policy Analysis* 4, no. 3 (Summer 1978): 369–392.
91. Lasswell, "The Policy Orientation," p. 16.
92. Lasswell and Kaplan, *Power and Society*, pp. xii and xxiv.
93. Abraham Kaplan, *American Ethics and Public Policy* (New York: Oxford University Press, 1963); and Lasswell, *A Pre-View of Policy Sciences*.
94. See Duncan MacRae, "Valuative Problems of Public Policy Analysis," in John C. Crecine, ed., *Research in Public Policy Analysis and Management* (Greenwich, CT: JAI Press, 1981), vol. 1, pp. 175–195; Martin Rein, "Value-Critical Policy Analysis," in Daniel Callahan and Bruce Jennings, eds., *Ethics, the Social Sciences, and Policy Analysis* (New York: Plenum, 1983), chap 5.
95. Charles E. Lindblom, "The Handling of Norms in Policy Analysis," in Paul A. Baran et al., eds., *The Allocation of Economic Resources* (Stanford, CA: Stanford University Press, 1959).
96. Douglas J. Amy, "Why Policy Analysis and Ethics Are Incompatible," *Journal of Policy Analysis and Management* 3, no. 4 (Summer 1984): 573–591.
97. Yehezkel Dror, "Muddling Through—'Science' or Inertia?" *Public Administration Review* 24, no. 3 (September 1964): 153–157; for a salient restatement, see Linder and Peters, "A Design Perspective on Policy Implementation."
98. Two excellent contributions to this conundrum are Frank

Fischer, *Politics, Values, and Public Policy* (Boulder, CO: Westview Press, 1980); and Martin Rein, *Social Science and Public Policy* (Baltimore: Penguin, 1976).

99. Douglas Yates, *Bureaucratic Democracy* (Cambridge, MA: Harvard University Press, 1982).

100. deLeon, "Policy Evaluation and Program Termination," p. 636; for support to this proposition, see Richard Nathan et al., *The Consequences of Cuts* (Princeton, NJ: Princeton University Press, 1983); and Lester M. Salamon and Michael W. Lund, eds., *The Reagan Presidency and the Governing of America* (Washington, DC: Urban Institute, 1984).

101. Quoted by Lee May, "U.S. Softens Urban Policy After Criticism," *Los Angeles Times*, July 10, 1982, p. 6.

102. Rochelle L. Stanfield, " 'If It Ain't Broke, Don't Fix It,' Say Defenders of Compensatory Aid," *National Journal* 14, no. 5 (January 30, 1982): 201; also Rochelle L. Stanfield, "Breaking Up the Education Department—School Aid May Be the Main Target," *National Journal* 13, no. 43 (October 24, 1981): 1907–1910.

103. The DOE sunset review is quoted by Burt Solomon, "DOE Memoirs to Congress," *Energy Daily* 10, no. 28 (February 11, 1982): 4. Also see Burt Solomon, "DOE: 'Give Me Death'," *Energy Daily* 10, no. 98 (May 25, 1982): 1, 4.

104. See, *inter alia*, George W. Downs and Patrick D. Larkey, *The Search for Government Efficiency* (New York: Random House, 1986), chap. 4; Dale Whittington and Duncan MacRae, Jr., "The Issue of Standing in Cost-Benefit Analysis," *Journal of Policy Analysis and Management* 5, no. 4 (Summer 1986): 665–682; and Michael S. Baram, "Cost-Benefit Analysis: An Inadequate Basis for Health, Safety, and Environmental Regulatory Decisionmaking," *Ecology Law Quarterly* 8 (1980): 473–531.

3 / Consent: Political Events and the Policy Sciences

A little more she strove and much repented,
And whispering "I will ne'er consent"—consented.

—George Gordon, Lord Byron
"Don Juan"

INTRODUCTION

The introductory chapter proposed the evolution of the policy sciences as a function of two broad sets of attributes and influences. The first set was characterized as composed of endogenous (or internal) variables, or those factors which defined and shaped the policy sciences concept and approach from within the area of inquiry. Described as "supply" or "advice" components, these included such influences as provided by the contributing disciplines (e.g., economics, sociology, and political science) and the explicit normative considerations embedded in the approach. For better or worse, these were largely brought to the policy sciences in a relatively disciplined although circumscribed manner by their practitioners.

The second set was described as the exogenous (or external) variables or forces as they affected the approach. These generally referred to political or contextual conditions which lay beyond the control of the analyst and often the decisionmaker. In most cases, they seemingly dictated the modes of analysis which were required by the tasks at hand. More crucially, they often determined if any analysis would even be performed. These were described as "demand" factors, that is, those forces which provided the opportunity for the application of the policy sciences approach to actual social problems that validated the problem-orientation criteria forwarded by its advocates.

This second set of influences is characterized by the consent of policymakers—however hesitantly or reluctantly—to permit societally relevant knowledge into the policy formulation, political decisionmaking, implementation, and evaluation circles on a routinized basis. More specifically, it attempts to define the policy sciences in the political environments in which they must operate by demonstrating how various contextual conditions—some might call them crises—have shaped the development of the approach. The explicit thesis of this perspective is that various demand phenomena—i.e., political events—have had fundamental—not evanescent—effects on the policy sciences. Implicit here is the assumption that subsequent political events can conceivably have just as great an effect. Therefore, to understand both the development and future of the policy sciences, one must examine the consent side of the expression.

One could, of course, quickly dismiss this proposition as trivial, one whose validity is so patent that it need not be tested. Policy is a manifestation of the political process and therefore must be embedded in the political process; ergo, it will surely and undoubtedly be affected by political events.[1] Although this argument has a certain validity, it should not necessarily be quietly accepted. Nor does it detail how political events might possibly shape the policy process in differential manners. Furthermore, being "right" does not mean that it is accepted. The historical record indicates that any number of policy studies have rated the techniques used over the recommendations reached, that is, exercised sophisticated disciplinary or methodological approaches with scant regard to the policy contexts or recommendations of the studies;[2] in Kaplan's incisive metaphor, "when all you have is a hammer, the whole world looks like a nail."[3]

While I do not wish to single out operations research (OR) as a particularly liable or visible offender, its early successes in such relatively bounded problems as the efficient distribution of goods or services in a constricted environment (e.g., allocation of emergency services in a given borough) gave OR proponents greater confidence in its capabilities than its later applications in more complex policy environments warranted. This tendency is especially apparent in the OR applications in urban problems, such as the optimal distributions of police and fire forces or school bus routings.[4] Similarly, reliance on the physical laws governing magnetic flux have been misleading in modeling fluctuations in urban land developments, a decided political arena.[5] It was only after the findings of the OR studies were devalued by the pressures of urban politics that their proponents began to appreciate the force of the political context in which their recommendations had to survive.

In short, excessive albeit understandable attention to the endogenous variables has often resulted in strictly disciplinary exercises with more of a policy veneer than a viable policy application. Political events, the contextual bone and sinew of the policy context, have been generally overlooked in the conceptual paradigms and applications. Such studies have adjured the multidisciplinary admonitions of the early policy sciences proponents. In so doing, they have effectively disregarded the political and social complexities which characterize public policy problems and, as a consequence, distanced their recommendations from potential policy relevance. Thus, one is motivated to explore carefully what some might term "obvious," for the obvious lessons seem to have been woefully neglected when many nominally policy-oriented studies based upon disciplinary research turn to real world policy problems.

There is, furthermore, a more subtle and persuasive reason for examining the stated thesis. While it is true—and maybe even occasionally accepted and practiced—that political conditions often determine the mode of analysis, the effects are usually treated as ad hoc or ephemeral. Each analysis is thought to be unique because of its peculiar political context. Therefore, each overlay of technique and context offers little in the way of cumulative learning.[6] This chapter directly denies this proposition and assumes as a working hypothesis that political events have sufficient similarities so that contextual analogs can be constructed, generalized, and transferred from one analytic situation to another. In doing so, it distinguishes between situations which are more or less relevant to the policymaker's problem at hand, and thereby distinguishes among competing analytic approaches.[7]

This is a critical distinction. Trends and conditions can be discerned and drawn for policy problem applications, but not without some dangers. George and his colleagues claim that President Johnson fundamentally misconstrued the "lessons" of the Cuban missile crisis in his gradual escalation of American military pressure against the North Vietnamese.[8] Likewise, one must be careful not to apply the remedies of Watergate to the wounds of the Iran-Contra affairs, even if both were constitutional corruptions perpetrated against the American political system. On the positive side, President Kennedy is generally acknowledged to have profited a great deal from his failures at the Bay of Pigs, which were to serve him well during the Cuban missile crisis. There is, then, a "learning curve," defined and drawn by historical events, from which both policy scientists and policymakers can benefit. Were this not the case, policymakers would be reduced to anecdotal evidence and an overreliance on personal experience.[9]

In line with this assumption is the hypothesis that there have been a number of political events of sufficient significance that they have actually molded the basic philosophy and approaches employed by the policy sciences as they are presently practiced. In a sentence, context counts. This chapter explores in a propositional way what some of these events were, how and why they affected the policy sciences, and what we might propose about future transformations of similar ilk and influence. Specifically, we will examine the effects of the following political events on the policy sciences:

- World War II
- the War on Poverty
- Vietnam
- Watergate
- the energy crises

These episodes, however disparate, share a common theme: they all offered tremendous opportunities for the policy sciences and their practitioners to develop their approaches and applications, for "lessons to be learned." In many cases, the positive opportunities were squandered, the relevant lessons generated from mistakes and shortcomings rather than triumphs and successes. Still, as we shall see, these historical events were essential in the molding of the policy sciences as they are described and practiced today.

THE CONTEXTUAL DEVELOPMENT OF THE POLICY SCIENCES

The previous chapter referred to a number of disciplinary advances during the twentieth century (remembering that the development of the policy sciences is principally a twentieth-century phenomenon) which provided methodological foundations for societally relevant knowledge. What was largely lacking in the first half of the century were the opportunities to apply this knowledge or, more relevantly, the recognition by policymakers that there were problems which could be usefully addressed by the social sciences on a routinized basis. Political contexts and events were needed to bring out these potentials. The following discussions of these events will be brief; their details are well known. More to the point is that they are being used here less as case histories and more to illustrate how they influenced the development of the policy sciences.

World War II

Seemingly, World War II provided the necessary ingredients to take the policy sciences out of the retired groves of academe into the turbulent circles of policymaking. Operations research provided a powerful set of quantitative tools applied to the war efforts;[10] indeed, Lineberry identifies Koopmans' uses of OR techniques for American transatlantic ship convoys as the first "identifiable" instance of policy analysis.[11] Social scientists assembled by the U.S. Library of Congress to study the wartime uses of propaganda developed and articulated many of the ideas that were later to surface as parts of the policy sciences.[12] The Office of Price Administration (OPA) and the War Production Board were examples of analytic agencies established to monitor the American economy and make specific recommendations towards improving the wartime industrial base and its production capabilities.[13] The OPA commissioned public opinion surveys to establish rationing policy. A team of psychologists in the Wartime Relocation Authority studied problems that arose with the decision to intern Japanese immigrants and Japanese-Americans. Drawing upon Robert Yerkes' pathbreaking use of intelligence testing during World War I, the Applied Psychology Panel employed standardized psychological testing procedures for selecting and assigning American service personnel, even though with only limited success.[14] The Office of Scientific Research and Development (OSRD) coordinated a number of weapons-related research projects, ranging from the atomic bomb to commando uses of bows and arrows.[15] Lastly, the collection, interpretation, and dissemination of intelligence information was emphasized by the formation of several analytic offices devoted to these activities by all the major combatants; code breaking (e.g., the British Ultra and the U.S. Navy's Purple endeavors) was the most famous example. These agencies quickly gained unprecedented access to the highest councils of military and political decisionmaking and, not surprisingly, great importance.[16]

Taken collectively, it is almost certain that these wartime agencies and their variegated efforts contributed immensely, maybe decisively, to the Allies' victory in World War II, though certainly not in equal amounts. They were a striking example of the relevance of problem-oriented research, although these were rarely multidisciplinary in nature.

The wartime analytic and organization experiences within the U.S. government, in retrospect, provided the stimulus and support for what was to emerge as directed, policy-oriented research, an inertia which carried into the immediate postwar era. It also revealed some notable cautions and obstacles, such as the gaping deficiencies in national data bases. Disciplinary theory was revealed to be ruefully inadequate, as Lyons recounts:

> The war also compelled economists of the traditional school to question some of their assumptions and reckon with advances in sociology and social psychology. The idea of rational self-interest as a prime economic force was especially doubtful in a period of total war, when administrative decisions largely replaced the free interplay of supply and demand in the market place.[17]

The Full Employment Act of 1947 created a formal Council of Economic Advisers (CEA) within the executive branch. Shortly thereafter, the government's responsibility to fund and foster scientific research was acknowledged by the founding of the National Science Foundation (NSF).[18] The congressional hearings on the NSF, a direct descendant of the OSRD, generated an intense and illustrative debate over the social function and accountability of government-sponsored scientific research.[19] The natural scientists, especially physicists flaunting their Manhattan Project credentials, were in the vanguard of the deliberations and the subsequent allocations of government largess. Support for the social sciences was considered but completely written out of the NSF-mandating legislation. Not surprisingly, their internal rigor and social relevance were the major issues in doubt.

In terms of policy research institutions, the Office of Naval Research was created to support basic scientific research, primarily conducted through universities. Drawing primarily upon the resources of the Douglas Aircraft Corporation and encouraged by a grant from the Ford Foundation, the Air Force established the RAND Corporation—subsequently characterized to be the prototypical "think tank"—as a source of independent policy analysis and recommendation. RAND quickly expanded beyond its physical and engineering sciences expertise to include a number of economists and political scientists in its research cadre.[20] At roughly the same time, Lerner and Lasswell coined the phrase "policy sciences" to define a distinct field of inquiry characterized by its problem-oriented concerns, multidisciplinary approach, and normative considerations.[21] Thus, a positive record of achievement and support springing from the World War II experiences and growing institutional havens appeared to be converging to the benefit of the policy sciences in the early 1950s.

In spite of this spate of activities, research explicitly designed and executed to advise the policymaker in a coherent and sustained intellectual and professional manner waned after its initial exposition in the early 1950s. Government sponsorship, so generous during the war years, all but disappeared in the face of Eisenhower's restricted budgets, a low government profile in most areas, and a series of economic recessions. Although there were policy-oriented research and analysis activities during the

1950s, they were largely isolated, nonrecurring, and consensual exercises which were unexceptional in their findings and recommendations. Even the Gaither and Rockefeller reports, which tolled the national security tocsin, were largely glossed over in terms of the recommendations that the Eisenhower administration chose to accept. Academic proponents, like Lasswell and Merton, would occasionally speak to the necessity of applying the social sciences to public policy questions,[22] but, for the most part, the intellectual and organizational impetuses that emanated from World War II became quiescent. Similarly, the demand from governmental sponsors and policymakers for these services withered on the vine, if not completely away.

The reason for the hiatus appears not to be one of conceptual lethargy or institutional deficiencies. Economists, legal scholars, public administrators, and political scientists had already made significant inroads into policy research, especially in the area of national security and, to a lesser extent, social welfare and unemployment. There were a handful of government offices, particularly within the Department of Defense, which could be described an analytic in their orientations. The Ford and Russell Sage foundations supported pioneering social research projects. And policy research organizations, such as the Brookings Institution, the RAND Corporation, and the Institute for Defense Analyses, conducted independent policy studies for an increasing number of clients on a growing list of topics. For example, RAND expanded beyond its Air Force origins to initiate studies for the Atomic Energy Commission. But these were exceptions. Most of this activity was politically insignificant because the larger political context did not call for—did not support—the development and application of policy-oriented research to perceived social problems. The demand did not match the supply. There was a perceived relative dearth of public sector problems to galvanize the policymaking communities into sponsoring policy research. The Eisenhower presidency, particularly during its first term, did not experience the types of political stresses which would have motivated organized policy research, let alone spark an entire cottage industry.

This is not to imply that the 1950s were a halcyonic period, one lacking political turmoil and debate; the Cold War, school desegregation, and recurring economic recessions would have apparently offered policy problems aplenty. However, the policymakers of the time seemingly did not think that these problems were amenable to the policy sciences approach, if indeed, they even knew such a thing existed. The innovative work of the analytic agencies and offices of World War II were apparently forgotten. For a lack of appropriate political stimuli and, secondarily, a corporate memory, the policy sciences were not able to build upon the openings and advances generated by the exigencies of World War II. A professional state of suspended animation prevailed. Still, the precedents had been set, a heritage established.

The War on Poverty

It took another "war" to stir the policy sciences out of their professional hibernation. Less violent than World War II, the American War on Poverty was much more influential in its effect on the development of the policy sciences. Poverty and poverty research had extensive roots in the United States but only fleeting, minor impacts on the public conscience and programs.[23] Now, charged by *Brown* v. *Board of Education,* the belated recognition of pervasive, pernicious racial discrimination, and journalistic accounts of degenerative, debilitating poverty in "the other America,"[24] the Kennedy and Johnson administrations moved aggressively to initiate and implement a wide variety of social welfare programs.[25] These efforts were accelerated by the destructive urban riots of the mid 1960s, as television brought the evidence of social injustices and inequities to the public's attention. Unquestionably well-intended, an avalanche of corrective programs were proposed and executed, ranging from education to housing to nutrition to employment.[26] New programs were initiated—such as Head Start, the Job Corps, and CETA—while existing programs were revitalized, especially under Social Security (e.g., Aid to Families with Dependent Children). In Nathan's recall, "Research was touted as a determinant in and of itself of new policy directions, or at least as an input with a presumed special claim and higher standing than others in the policymaking process. This was the highwater mark for policy-oriented social science."[27]

The common thread of these programs, unfortunately unrecognized at the time, was profound ignorance, of both the cause of the social malaise they were to alleviate and their possible consequences. More telling was the lack of clear or even consensual objectives. Unbridled enthusiasm, motivated by political drive, supplanted whatever meager analysis was available; in Moynihan's apt phrase, the War on Poverty programs were based on "maximum feasible misunderstanding."[28] The result, not surprisingly, was a decade of trial, error, and frustration, after which it was arguable if ten years and billions of dollars had produced any discernible, let alone effective, reliefs.[29] Indeed, Murray's later assessment asserts that the people the programs were designed to help were actually worse off than they had been prior to these programs, that relative to the baseline white populations, black Americans were "losing ground."[30]

The results of the War on Poverty were controversial and problematic. Its effects on the policy sciences could be similarly characterized. The difference is that the war's imprint upon the policy sciences was far more lasting than its ability to relieve American poverty and discrimination. From the conceptual, methodological, and political perspectives, the War on Poverty produced fundamental alterations in the fledgling policy sciences. Root causes—was poverty due to structural, cultural, or economic deficiencies?—rather than simple surface symptoms were debated. More important, actual programs were established as a result of those deliberations.[31] The "lessons learned" were largely of the "mistakes to be avoided" variety, applicable to all phases of policy analysis activities. The initiation of many programs was ill-informed, innovation being the foundling of political necessity rather than analysis and information. Implementation was ignored as an unimportant afterthought, naively left to supposedly neutral administrators and bureaucrats. Program evaluation was neglected until much too late and then discovered to be theory, methodology, and data bereft; it served little constructive purpose. In short, poverty's social maladies were found to be much more complex than previously realized, therefore staunchly resistant to the social scientists' remedies.[32] When they compared the promised with the delivered products, both practitioners and sympathetic sponsors became skeptical regarding the ability of the policy analysts to alleviate social problems.[33] Admission of policy researchers into policymaking circles had proven extremely problematic for the former and highly dubious for the latter.

The influence of the War on Poverty on the policy sciences can be seen in many reactions, subsequent themes, and general reservations. On the most practical level, it provided social scientists with heretofore unheard of amounts of financial support (from both public and private sources) and ready access to policymakers. Neither reward, of course, is trivial; combined, they yielded a heady if not well-warranted brew. On the more conceptual level, partially stimulated and illustrated by the War on Poverty experiences, a major outpouring of policy-oriented literature appeared in the late 1960s and early 1970s.[34] In many instances—perhaps in zealous anticipation, perhaps in renewed enthusiasm, perhaps in vested self-interest—some proponents grossly exaggerated the promise of the policy sciences: Dror might have been an outspoken but hardly isolated voice when he proclaimed that the "policy sciences must integrate knowledge from a variety of branches of knowledge into a supradiscipline focusing on public policymaking."[35] Professional journals were started and several universities (most notably, Harvard and the University of California, Berkeley) established professional graduate training and doctoral programs in public policy analysis. Even the *New York Times* took note.[36] In many ways, opportunity seemingly created an unlimited demand; consent was the order of the day. Policy analysis rocketed in the bureaucratic "policy space," even though its objectives and destinations were unknown and its means uncertain.

Not unexpectedly, the inevitable morning after exposed a loss of innocence and mutual respect between the practitioner and the sponsor. Policy researchers had to swallow twin bitter pills of methodological deficiency and result failure. Theoretical assumptions which had proven so convincing in academic conventions were revealed to be inadequate bases for devising effective social intervention programs. Questions regarding the measurement of the quality of education or the application of labor economics to unemployment and poverty were found to be much more complex—perhaps even intractable—to answer than previously imagined.[37] Social welfare programs often were structured upon incentives which undermined their basic objectives, thus ensuring their ineffectiveness.[38] Empirical research, such as portended by systems analysis and welfare economics, foundered on the shoals of inadequate data, social complexities, and practical realities. Most pointedly, the political parameters which defined and motivated the War on Poverty programs were distinctly seen as both an inherent part of the policy problem and, therefore, an integral part of any problem solution. Research which denied or neglected this condition on either side of the problem or solution expression was doomed to be frustrating and disappointing. While this contextual fact of life had been nominally recognized by the systems analysis and economics heritages of the policy sciences, the War on Poverty brought this lesson unequivocally home.

As was the case with the previous war, the reagent for the policy sciences' prominence was the contextual events occasioned by political exigencies. The War on Poverty provided unprecedented opportunity for the policy sciences to win their professional and disciplinary laurels, "a Camelot for the social sciences."[39] For whatever reasons, these opportunities were not successfully seized. Rather than kudos, the War on Poverty left the policy sciences with ample evidence for professional humility and an imperative for considerable intellectual retrenchment.

Vietnam

The predominant political event of the 1960s in the United States was the conflict in Vietnam. Closely monitored by Presidents Johnson, Nixon, and Ford, the analysis and conduct of the war were the responsibilities of the Office of the Secretary of Defense (OSD) and the military services. In a sense, Vietnam could have been the foundry and mettle of "rational" analysis, for the defense community had consistently been at the forefront of analytic approaches. Systems analysis and costing techniques had been developed by the RAND Corporation under the sponsorship of the Air Force and OSD.[40] The "economics of defense" were well articulated, if not always well practiced.[41] It should be no surprise that the Program Planning Budgeting System (PPBS) was first implemented within the Defense Department. Yet, in hindsight, it can be argued that with all its apparent analytic prowess, the United States profoundly mismanaged—or, more bluntly, lost—

the Vietnam war, even if, as Gelb and Betts write, the irony is that the policy system "worked."[42] Gray takes the argument one step further, contending that one of the major shortcomings of the American war effort and a root cause for its futility was the reliance upon analytic techniques; Brodie, in an article commissioned to refute Gray's charges, ends up in basic agreement.[43]

Without pausing here to reflect upon the controversies and failures of the American involvement in and conduct of the Vietnam war, one can easily point to inadequacies in information transmission, faulty analogies, reluctance to include social and political variables (and a concomitant commitment to quantitative measures), and incremental decisionmaking as contributory factors that undermined the analysis which rationalized the conduct of the Vietnam war.[44] This set of charges had important readings for the policy analysis communities.

Policymakers and analysts could have extracted at least five critical "lessons" from Vietnam. First, it was realized that purely "rational" decisionmaking was decidedly deficient in the political fora. This was especially apparent during the Vietnam conflict, one waged between participants with significantly different cultures and value structures. The resolve of the North Vietnamese consistently violated the logical bases upon which U.S. analysts recommended and policymakers justified their decisions to escalate the war against Hanoi. Second, quantitative measures were seen as being unreliable for planning purposes. In fact, later disclosures revealed that the numbers coming out of Vietnam were just as subjective and open to manipulation as the more explicitly political or interpretative reports. The cognitive and operational models employed were often irrelevant to the actual war effort. Third, the conservative nature of policy analysis reinforced the commitment to the incremental nature of American decisionmaking, thus making a major departure from existing policy an alternative advanced only by those out of favor or court (e.g., Deputy Secretary of State George Ball). The slow pace of the war—both in escalation and deescalation—permitted domestic critics to coalesce and eventually shut down the war efforts, but only after horrendous losses of life.

Fourth, Vietnam was a constantly altered arena, a contextual chameleon which defied static analysis. Yet most contemporary

American interpretations of the conflict refused to countenance the changing political landscape until the evidence was inescapable and only radical remedies remained. This realization moved the policy profession away from its assumptions that contextual conditions were relatively stable and towards a working inclusion of a dynamic set of trends and situations. For example, American domestic tolerances of the war were constantly changing and ultimately affected the conduct of a war half-a-world away. Finally, the Vietnam war demonstrated just as forcefully as the War on Poverty the normative imperatives, especially in terms of objectives and goals, that must be articulated in any major policy analysis. Motivations, such as U.S. commitment and credibility (the key buzz words of their day), were central to the American involvement but were relegated to undefined analytic impotence by the more measurable logistics flows, enemy defections, and body counts. Whereas some vague political consensus might have supported (or acquiesced in) U.S. policy during the early days of the Vietnam war, the eroding political base—sapped by the growing public conviction that the war was morally reprehensible—was not acknowledged in the executive branch boardrooms until student riots and election results were manifested in the American social and political circles.

All of these conditions required the more conscientious policy scientists to amend their confidences in systems and quantitative analyses, not to place all their analytic eggs in one basket. This is not to suggest that quantitative methodologies were tossed aside like last year's alchemies or that "situational ethics" became the new touchstone, but one can argue that the contextual experiences of Vietnam produced a greater appreciation for the human and normative elements embedded in the policy processes. Hence, the Vietnam experiences urged a new mix between the quantitative and qualitative aspects of policymaking, with a greater emphasis on the latter than might previously have been the case.

Watergate

In time, it is possible that the forced resignations of President Richard Nixon and Vice President Spiro Agnew as a result of the

Watergate and related disclosures may be perceived as little more than an unfortunate but inconsequential contretemps in American politics, an ill-conceived and badly handled venture that mushroomed into prominence more because of the subsequent cover-up machinations than the criminal acts themselves.[45] The American body politic responded as one might hope to the inexcusable signs of political corruption and flagrant abuses of power. The offending tumors were effectively and publicly excised and—from a functional perspective—quickly replaced, all within the bounds of legitimacy and with no malingering toxins. Q.E.D. End of episode.

This would be a shallow reading. Watergate was a milestone in the public awareness of government, probably a more visible phenomenon to the majority of the American people than the War on Poverty, especially as it raised the explicit and uncomfortable issue of morality in government. Few will forget President Nixon incredibly protesting "I am not a crook" prior to his resignation, Vice President Agnew abjectly bargaining before submitting a plea of *nolo contendere* to accepting illegal contributions, or Alexander Butterfield advising young people not to enter the public service. Political corruption and a patent misuse of power were impressed indelibly upon the American public.[46] While the moral courage of Eliot Richardson and Archibald Cox, victims of the "Saturday Night Massacre," suggested that scruples were not totally absent from government, the overall and justifiable public impression of the Watergate episode was one of scurrilous and immoral behaviors throughout the executive branch of the government, up to and including its highest offices. The public's repugnance to the Watergate activities was demonstrated by Congress's vote to bring impeachment proceedings against President Nixon, and, later, by the electorate's rejection of President Ford's bid for reelection, a choice at least partially motivated by Ford's decision to grant Nixon a presidential pardon.

Even though the actual effects of Watergate on the American political system may have been transitory (the Ethics in Government Act of 1978 being the most visible remnant), its surfacing of the issue of political rectitude and morality added new evidence to the admonishments of the early policy sciences proponents who had urged the explicit consideration of normative standards as a central criterion of the policy sciences approach and the operating policy process. Watergate conferred a new legitimacy and urgency on those concerns while, at the same time, stoking the debate as to how morality and value judgments could, in practical ways, be incorporated in a policy exercise or even academic policy curricula.

Unlike the previous examples of political conditions which provided the policy sciences with significant new opportunities in terms of problem-oriented research or multidisciplinary approaches, the political contexts of Watergate provided substantial cause for the policy sciences to reassess and renew their commitment to norms and values. No longer would it be admissible for the analyst to protest "I could do it but it would be wrong."

The Energy Crises

The 1973 and 1978 energy crises in the United States and their feared economic and social ramifications all but dictated that energy supplies would be a major analytic focus and, more important, political issue throughout the 1970s. To help unravel the complicated relationships between energy resources and uses, public and private sponsors generated an immense series of research studies, most of them quantitative in nature, which were used as the basis for recommending and formulating energy policy.[47] A good many of these studies were based upon elaborate computer models in which complex networks of interacting mathematical equations attempted to simulate the reaction of the economy given different energy supply and demand levels. Variables included the price of oil and other energy sources (e.g., nuclear, renewable, and synthetic fuels), demand rates, and allocations of energy among various end use sectors (e.g., industry versus residential versus transportation), all over different time frames. Mathematical models were the principal tool of investigation, even though an earlier survey of federally funded modeling exercises concluded that "perhaps as many as two-thirds of the models failed to achieve their avowed purposes in the form of direct application to policy problems."[48]

The analyses were hardly academic or moot in their policy implications. As gas lines stretched and public tempers shortened, relatively technical energy studies could be found in local book stores, one even becoming a best seller.[49] The energy crises were the cause of major institutional upheavals in Washington: the Atomic Energy Commission dissolved into the Energy Research and Development Agency which, in turn, became the cabinet-level Department of Energy. President Nixon mandated "Project Independence"; President Carter wore sweaters, urged energy conservation, subsidized the solar energy and synthetic fuels industries, and declared the energy crisis the "moral equivalency of war." To a few observers, it might have been more than a moral equivalency, as some advocated U.S. military intervention in the Middle East in light of the precarious situation posed by the Western reliance on the Persian Gulf nations' oil reserves.[50] War or not, the energy crisis presented the types of political exigencies and disputes which might well have been a gold mine for the development, access, and use of the policy sciences and their methodologies.

To be more specific, the energy crises were characterized by at least four features as they apply to the policy sciences which merit review. First, beyond the generic rallying call for "energy independence," there was little agreement across the energy community upon goals, let alone the appropriate means to those objectives. Opposing camps were formed that were at constant loggerheads because they had little in common except their implacable opposition to one another. Renewable versus nuclear energy was the most strident dyad. The basic assumptions, analytical frameworks, methodological approaches, energy supply and demand projections, and even what constituted acceptable data (and their sources) of the different stakeholders were so incompatible that no dialogue or policy convergence should have been expected. Robinson relates how the contending stakeholders could not even compare apples with oranges; rather, they were talking apples versus horned toads.[51] The controversies between the contending "tribes" were later described as "examples not of decisionmaking under uncertainty but of decisionmaking under contradictory certainties."[52] It was little wonder then that no coherent national energy policy was articulated, let alone executed.

Second, there was an abiding distrust of virtually everything connected with the energy crisis. The public perceived the oil companies as reaping "obscene profits," the Arabs as the "bad guys," and government officials as mindlessly meddlesome "middlemen." More outspoken observers merely viewed everybody tainted with energy analysis or policy as either incompetent or fraudulent. Any policy exercise had to be played out in an extremely fractious political arena, a chastening experience for the analysts heretofore cloistered in analytic havens or bureaucratic backwaters.

Third, there were in fact fundamental technical uncertainties, even unknowables, which clouded the analysis and fueled the disputes. Under the best of computational circumstances, the difficulties of accurately estimating supply and demand levels for energy resources and applications would be monumental. In the politically virulent environment of the energy crises, they were insurmountable.[53] This situation was exacerbated by the government's heavy-handed manipulation of the energy simulation models, constantly tweaked until they produced results which supported predetermined political positions.[54] Distressingly, these manipulations were hidden behind the guise of objective quantitative modeling by their very designers, people who certainly knew better. Many of these computer models were briefed to, employed by, and relied upon by policymakers who lacked the technical background to evaluate them; what reservations they might have had were more intuitive than informed. Yet there is good reason to believe that the model results, however imperfect or specious, were used to devise and support national energy policy.[55]

Fourth, the energy crises had tremendous public visibility and effect. They left nobody's life untouched and were seen to portend more dire consequences if left unattended. Solutions were not available but "something" had to be done to placate public sentiment. Energy models were seen by policymakers as low-cost political actions or ready symbols of government attention to these threats, a relatively quick and costless "fix," as it were. Symbols were substituted for substance.[56]

Taken in total, the energy crises presented a symbiotic relationship between policy analysts and policymakers, a condition fraught with significant opportunities and pitfalls for the policy sciences. Both were extravagantly sampled to no one's particular gain.

As implied above, the energy crises presented policy analysts with the chance to parade their technical modeling skills before the highest councils of government. Their findings could define and determine policy. Furthermore, they could be assertive in their analyses because it was obvious that the policymakers did not have the technical expertise to assess (i.e., accept or reject) their work. Together, this was an intoxicating condition, but it forced a genuine dilemma upon the energy analyst. There was ample evidence that quantitative models had nowhere near the forecasting precisions ascribed to them by their advocates.[57] At the same time, the putatively "objective" nature of the modeling exercises and their computational opaqueness concealed the reality that their underlying and usually unspoken political and social assumptions were what actually "drove" the results. These shortcomings presented a tension with the energy analysis community between honesty and access. Rather than confess to the limitations of their approaches, the energy acolytes presented their computer projections with undeserved confidences and hidden caveats. Although these were matters of some debate, to admit to these (at best) ambiguities would have severely curtailed the analysts' newly won and treasured entree to lofty ambiences of power.

To be fair, the duplicity was hardly one-sided. Cognizant policymakers were rarely reluctant to dictate desired model results to technicians which would support their predetermined positions.[58] The point here is distinctly negative in tone: the analytic commitment to the responsible reporting of methodologies and results was sorely strained during the energy crises, a professional dereliction which served neither party's long-range purposes.

As was the case with the previous "wars," the energy crises' studies reinforced the need for multidisciplinary approaches, even in the presence (or perhaps because) of massive quantitative computer models. This is particularly illustrative because so many of the elements of the energy crises seemed to be "technical" in nature (e.g., future energy demands levels and untapped petroleum reserves). But the "objective" nature of energy was more façade than fact. Simple aggregation of assumed individual demand preferences did not translate into reliable national energy demand projections. An overreliance on the "technology assessment" model rendered congressional energy analysts relatively insensitive to the relationship between technology and social change.[59] The political motivations and actions of the OPEC nations distanced any analysis of energy supplies from the comfortable calculus of economic supply and demand. The interaction of the public and private sectors and the dynamics of technology diffusions required still another set of disciplinary perspectives beyond standard petroleum engineering and marketplace economics.[60] Legal and ecological issues had to be taken into account, as well as philosophical preferences. These aspects were best mirrored in the centralized versus decentralized and "hard" versus "soft" energy dichotomies.[61] The convoluted contextuality of the energy debate clearly required that the policy sciences retire whatever vestiges of strictly disciplinary research they might still have retained.

A final lesson for the policy sciences from the energy crises of the 1970s was the necessity to be able to translate sophisticated, technical analysis into language policymakers and the public at large could assimilate and to couch recommendations in the political environs in which policymakers must operate.[62] This surely was not an unprecedented observation; analyst-client communications have been a repeated theme in the policy analysis literature.[63] But rarely has the requirement been so starkly posed and left unrequited. This could have been a mixed blessing, for some of the energy studies achieved prominence more as a result of their self-generated publicity than for the quality of their research and recommendations. Complex situations were reduced to simplistic and misleading bromides. This was much too true during the energy crises when relevance and rigor were not necessarily reinforcing, let alone complementary. Especially during politically volatile situations, policy articulation is a delicate yet critical balance of conveying the complex in understandable terms which needs to be firmly incorporated into the policy sciences' practice.

Overall, the energy crises forced what could be described as a set of insoluble analytic and policy problems upon the energy community and the overall public. No single policy could have accommodated and coordinated all the contending factions, which is probably why no overarching national energy policy was ever formulated. Indeed, many claim that most government programs, such as energy subsidies and gasoline rationing, only skewed the market and worsened the situation. Furthermore, there was no clean, identifiable end to the energy crises,* such as marked the termination of World War II, Vietnam, or Watergate. Thus, any review of the energy crises is problematic. But these caveats should not obscure the multiple failures of commission and omission of the energy policy analysts when they were given broad license to display their wares.

Lastly, whether the "lessons learned" from the energy crises' analytic shortcomings demonstrated during this period will be taken to professional and disciplinary heart is a particularly pertinent concern because of one key difference between the energy crises and the other political events described above: it is highly likely that the United States will experience another seriously debilitating energy shortfall; the only outstanding questions are of magnitude and timing.[64] The final judgment regarding the effect of the energy crises on the policy sciences can therefore be postponed until the next energy crisis, at which time the energy analysis and policymaking communities can draw upon their performance of the 1970s and perhaps redeem themselves. If this scenario does play, then maybe the energy follies and foibles of the 1970s may have been worth the price of admission. Still, one worries.

ON SECOND THOUGHT

Under most conventions of exposition, the final section of a chapter summarizes the preceding arguments, gingerly tests the posed hypotheses, and occasionally presents a set of stirring validations. We must momentarily set aside the accepted ground rules in order to admit to the tentative nature of the presented analysis and

---

*In this context, the use of the word "crisis" is semantically troublesome, since by definition, a crisis occurs in a time frame with an identifiable beginning and end; i.e., there cannot be a permanent "crisis."

observations. At least four epistemological reservations must be confessed. First, the objectives of this chapter might be sufficiently clear, but the means could be construed as disturbingly less than convincing to the neutral observer. The selective nature of the evidence certainly opens the analysis to question. Second, if we can grant that some political events have had noticeable effects on the concepts and practices of the policy sciences, then we are obligated to ask why other political exigencies have had little or, more fairly, less influence. Why ascribe effects to Watergate and not to the decision to use the atomic bomb? To the War on Poverty and not to the Great Depression? What about the Cuban missile crisis, the environmental protests, or the civil rights movement? Furthermore, even if we accept that event alpha had a greater impact than event beta, the next and most insistent question is why? What differentiates alpha from beta? Third, this discussion presupposes agreement on what constitutes "effect" and/or the duration of the changes. Fourth, the development of the policy sciences reflects the symbiotic relationship between the available intellectual tools and the contextual opportunities. The policy sciences could not prosper and mature without both. However, in this and the preceding chapter, the two have been presented as separate conditions. In so doing, I may have implied a biased or distorted view. There is, in short, a welter of definitional and evidential riddles which renders any observations problematic and must be frontally addressed.

Having entered the confessional and registered the appropriate *mea culpas,* let us now turn to their absolution. This implies a three-part penitence. First, we must address the question of the extent or significance of the political events as they affected the policy sciences. That is, we need to ask what constitutes a change or development. Next, we need to examine why some events or political contexts have seemingly had a greater effect on the evolution of the policy sciences than others. This will lead to the third task, that of discerning themes and harmonies which possibly conjoin the intellectual and contextual elements of policy research. These would be analogous to what Wildavsky refers to as the cogitation and social interaction components of policy analysis.[65] We turn immediately to the first two tasks; the third will be the subject of the next chapter.

What Changes?

The answer to the central question of what constitutes a fundamental change in the policy sciences approach must almost certainly be arbitrary or, more generously, a matter of degree. There is no available parallel to the touchstone transition in physics from Newton to Einstein or the Crick-Watson breakthroughs in molecular biology. One analyst's quantum could be another's increment. However, one can assert that major conceptual and organizational milestones have been posited and realized. For instance, the definition of the policy orientation approach, although growing upon early disciplinary contributions, was a marked departure from its antecedent intellectual activities.[66] Likewise, the establishment and support of "think tanks" were organizationally different from the transitory existences of earlier policy research commissions.[67] These distinctions might become more obscure, however, when one examines the significance of the ascribed effects across a broad range of policy issues. Also, the general burgeoning and diffusion of the policy sciences and policy analysis in the 1970s makes the uniform measure of such effects impossible, even if one could settle on a set of professional benchmarks.[68] The porridge thickens, for this raises the question of who "learns" or assimilates the putative "lessons." Moreover, are the "lessons" really learned and accepted within the policy sciences framework and communities, given their disparate nature and purposes? Are they true cachets or empty shibboleths? The IIASA energy model[69] has been criticized as being methodologically more suspect than its energy model predecessors of the 1970s.[70] Although the IIASA modelers certainly understood the faults and failures of the earlier energy models, the "lessons" they could have derived from them seemingly fell on deaf ears.

Still, it is possible to identify five fundamental effects upon the policy sciences which have been supported, perhaps even demanded, by political events and which have been assimilated (some more readily, some more completely than others) by the policy research communities. These are:

- increased resources, support, and acceptance
- multidisciplinary approaches
- increased public exposure

- normative consideration and analysis
- qualitative analysis

The most clear-cut effect of political events upon policy research has been the routine acceptance of formalized policy analysis within the councils of government and, more concretely, the accompanying financial and organizational support. The analytic and policy offices of World War II set the precedents for institutionalized government analysis. Although many of the wartime agencies and their studies disappeared with the end of the war, their memory and influence lingered. When the political demands for analysis resurfaced during the 1960s, the opportunities were not missed. Government largess veritably established and sustained a growth industry, resulting in support well beyond the expectations and capabilities of the existing policy research community. Universities, think tanks, profit-making research companies, and policy entrepreneurs expanded their size, scope, and client bases almost exponentially. Virtually every government organization created and staffed its own policy research branch, often predicated upon the Department of Defense model and methodologies (e.g., PPBS), with little attention to their applicability to the particular institutional sensitivities or policy areas. Congress mandated its own analytic agencies, the Congressional Budget Office and the Office of Technology Assessment, to shore up its analytic requirements. Like any unplanned sprawl, this uncontrolled expansion presented mixed blessings: policy research suddenly had heretofore unimagined resources, access, and organizational support; at the same time, it had an undisciplined, all-too-often unskilled number of practitioners. Regardless of this dilemma and its consequences, one can hardly dispute that the political events of World War II and the War on Poverty contributed to an unparalleled growth opportunity for policy research.

A second effect of political contexts upon the policy sciences was the insistence on multidisciplinary research. This, of course, was nothing new; it was one of the founding conditions of the problem-oriented research approach. But the nominal prescription and actual application of multidisciplinary analysis were widely divergent and long in coming. During most of the 1950s and 1960s, ongoing policy research studies were largely and firmly entrenched in a single approach, such as systems analysis, or discipline, most likely economics. For instance, a RAND Corporation study examined the effectiveness of education from the perspective of an economist's production function,[71] and many of the early evaluation studies were conducted by social psychologists and public health specialists.[72] The broad contextual demands placed upon the policy sciences by the War on Poverty, the energy crises, and the Vietnam engagement did more than "rediscover" the multidisciplinary urging of Lasswell, Dror, and Merton. In conjunction with the intellectual developments which stressed the importance of interdisciplinary research for advances in the social sciences,[73] the real world complexities posed by political events, which recognized no disciplinary boundaries, forced the widespread and general acceptance of multidisciplinary research. It is, of course, fair to ask if this interdisciplinary convergence would not have occurred in the normal ebb and flow of academic interests, yet there is little reason to doubt that the undisciplined and insistent world of policy problems added a shotgun element to what might have otherwise been a reluctant courtship and questionable consummation.

The third major change in the policy sciences' approach was the realization that its practitioners could no longer operate in a sequestered environment. Early problem-oriented research was, for a number of reasons, limited to a very small community (in many cases, just the analyst and the policymaker), a closed set at the preference of most of the participants. The emergence of policy research from the sheltered groves of academe and government offices into the lighted arenas of public debate removed that insularity. Most policy researchers have acknowledged that they can no longer whisper into a single ear. Therefore, their analyses must be conducted so that they can withstand independent scrutiny and verification. Although some might question the value of "sunshine" analysis and decisionmaking, this openness can only improve the quality of the process and the product.[74]

Furthermore, policy analysts must be able to couch their recommendations in ways that can be understood by both the responsive policymaker and the now-enlarged attentive public audience. The American failures in Vietnam can be partially attributed to the defense analysts' and policymakers' consistent reticence to include the American public as part of the relevant policy audience. Energy advisers during the 1970s were similarly guilty but in different ways. Some chose to popularize their arguments, making the complex look simple, thereby conveying a distorted picture of the problem and its potential solutions. Watergate would never have happened if its perpetrators had publicly disclosed their deliberations, or even opened their discussions to a wider circle of confidants.[75] Lastly, political events such as Vietnam and the energy crises convinced the public that it could and should involve itself in policy debates, even if the controversies appear, at first blush, to be forbidding and inappropriate for public discourse. The energy debates were staggeringly technical in tone, but since they intimately affected individual lives (e.g., the costs of residential heating), many citizens became knowledgeable—in effect, their own energy analysts.

This situation has sustained itself in other areas of public interest. Education and public health have long been areas of close public attention; the issues of English as a second language and AIDS are descendants of such concerns. The public perception of the imminent dangers of nuclear war has torn down the veils of secrecy and jargon which long excluded nuclear strategy from the public purview and effectively forced strategic analysts to make their work accessible and understandable.[76] Technical analyses of ecological and environmental proposals are commonly debated and adjudicated in public fora.

This trend towards openness surely benefited from the political events which demanded it. Lacking the political imperatives, policy researchers might well have continued in their relatively secluded ways, well cloistered in universities, research organizations, and government agencies, with only the occasional (and then disbarred) heretic choosing to "go public." There are, in many cases, good reasons for this isolation;[77] hue and cry rarely contribute to sound analysis. But for public policy debates set in a democratic society, these arguments have proven to be less than acceptable. The lessons were brought convincingly to light by the political contexts of Watergate, Vietnam (in particular, the publication of *The Pentagon Papers*), and the energy crises. Policy analysts must now assume that they—or at least their works—are part of the public record and domain.

The fourth major effect of these political events was the acceptance of the normative component of public policy within policy research. Again, this element had been stressed by the policy science pioneers. Lasswell wrote that "the policy sciences approach . . . calls forth a very considerable clarification of the value goals involved in policy."[78] However, even more than multidisciplinary research, these tenets were honored more in their breach than application. Lindblom wondered as to their importance, but in any case claimed that they could be safely incorporated in an incremental fashion;[79] many admitted that values might be important but could not be built into any rigorous analysis; but most simply chose to ignore the issue.

The political crises and events of the War on Poverty, Vietnam, and Watergate firmly displaced these conveniences. While a debate still continues as how to *best* incorporate norms into analysis,[80] there appears to be little disagreement that somehow they must be explicitly acknowledged and incorporated.[81] Rein refers to "value-critical analysis" as the next major advancement in policy research, and Wildavsky talks about the cultural components of policy research.[82] A major caution: since public values, almost by definition, are (and even ought to be) situational—that is, subject to change—and relative,[83] one can justifiably wonder as to the durability of this particular condition. The same American public opinion which demanded the resignation of Richard Nixon essentially readmitted him to the pantheon of power less than a decade later. Still, one need not require the permanence of a particular set of values to accept the argument that the explicit inclusion of norms and ethics into the policy sciences protocol has been partially encouraged by the political events of the last two decades.

Finally, the evaluations of many antipoverty programs and the increased recognition of the limitations of economic modeling, systems analysis, and cost-benefit analysis as estimating techniques have had a methodological effect on the policy analysis community. The awareness was reinforced by the failures of the massive energy models. The initial emphasis on quantitative measures was deeply shaken by the realization that there were severe fissures between theory, data, and the relevant social contexts.[84] This trend was substantiated by the growing realization that even in economic matters, quantitative analyses yielded problematic policy recommendations and, even more embarrassingly, programs which worsened rather than improved the situation. The Vietnam experiences cast additional doubts upon quantitative analysis; the War on Poverty was consistently hampered by a basic inability to estimate accurately the number of people who could be considered poverty-stricken and therefore eligible for the Great Society programs. And, finally, the apparent political manipulation of simple numbers, let alone numerical analysis, practiced during Vietnam, the War on Poverty, and the energy crises effectively laid to rest whatever visions might have remained regarding the "objectivity" or "neutrality" of quantitative analysis.

Combined with the admission that qualitative (e.g., social, legal, political, institutional, and environmental) elements were essential in any comprehensive analysis, the quantitative-qualitative mix which had been so decidedly quantitative in practice slowly began to redress itself. Moreover, it became clear that no ubiquitous model or single proportion would be right for all analyses. These new and still shifting analytic equilibria were made apparent and necessary when their earlier and more quantitative kin were revealed by the workaday political contexts in which they were immersed to be inadequate for their stated public policy purposes.

In summary, this review of the possible convergence of the intellectual and political threads of the policy sciences tapestry has argued how the latter has had a significant cognitive, structural, and operational effect upon the former. There have been, of course, a larger number of more marginal changes, such as the greater appreciation for the dynamic (as opposed to static) nature of policy problems,[85] but these are of less concern here. This admission, however, does not detract from the argument that the overall effect of specific political events upon the policy sciences has been discernible and telling.

What Events?

If one can accept that certain political events have had palpable effects on the development of the policy sciences, it stands to reason that other political events have had lesser effect. Certainly the political contexts accompanying World War I, the Great Depression and the subsequent New Deal programs, the Truman Doctrine and Marshall Plan, and the national security debates of the late 1940s and early 1950s provided sufficient cause and material to prime the policy sciences pump. And none would question that these were political events of the first magnitude, just as politically potent in their import as those events reviewed above. Yet the following brief narratives suggest that they had a relatively negligible role in the evolution of the policy sciences compared with the first set of historical incidents. Assuming that this is true, one is therefore moved to ask: Why is this the case? Why does one set of political contexts appear so much more influential than another? Without an answer to this question, one is left with a pedestrian description rather than an understanding of the development of the policy sciences.

As Lasswell and Lyons point out, social scientists, especially pyschologists and economists, made important contributions to the U.S. war effort in World War I.[86] But their experiences were somewhat isolated and were mostly set aside until World War II. This attitude was fostered by the general reluctance of the federal government to involve its offices in social problems, i.e., a minimal interventionist philosophy and posture. Given this stance, there was little reason for the government to encourage problem-oriented research. The precise reasons for this hiatus are uncertain, but they can generally be attributed to the lack of political demand for policy-oriented or applied social science research in the immediate postwar decades and the still-insecure relationship between the social sciences and problem-oriented research. While there were assuredly advocates of this relationship (e.g., Merriam and the Spellman and Rockefeller foundations), the interwar period was largely characterized by a consolidation of the intellectual tools being sharpened by economists, psychologists and political scientists within the ivy-covered walls of their respective disciplines. For whatever reasons, whatever problem-oriented research traditions that might have emerged from World War I languished between the wars.

Seemingly, the emergencies of the Great Depression and the resulting New Deal programs should have motivated and supported a thriving policy research field. The political and social conditions produced by the stock market crash and the economic depression and its unprecedented numbers of unemployed should have been license for policy research and programs, but those activities that were undertaken were temporary, almost admittedly band-aid in application and nature. Action rather than analysis was the key.[87] The virtually experimental character of many of the New Deal programs (witness the National Recovery Act) and agencies (e.g., the Civilian Conservation Corps) and the informal (although not insignificant) stature of Roosevelt's Brain Trust underpin this observation. There surely was a critical mass of concerned scholars and opportunity for policy research, but as a sustained activity with continued institutional support, there was little evidence of a coherent policy sciences enclave in government circles during and after the Great Depression. Perhaps the crises were too great and the demand too pressing to permit a more contemplative, studied approach; but except in isolated instances, there was surprisingly little in the way of policy research during this period, and certainly little research that resulted in specific public programs. In fairness, some New Deal agencies with analytic charters—such as the Security and Exchange Commission and the Tennessee Valley Authority—did continue into the postwar years, but these were exceptions. On the more positive side, one might argue that the experiences of the Great Depression did serve the policy sciences campaign because, in later years, researchers could look back at the missed opportunities and claim "If only. . . ." But, at best, this would be little more than a minor victory.

The Truman Doctrine and its enabling Marshall Plan were both the result of the immediate postwar crisis with the Soviet Union; the war had been won, but peace was yet to be found.[88] The Truman administration was convulsed by what to do in the face of the perceived Communist threat to Europe. State Department personnel authored numerous contingency papers, Congress was consulted, and American policy formulated and then executed. In many ways, the development of the Marshall Plan was a role model in policy innovation and implementation, just as instructive as the much-chronicled Cuban missile crisis. Yet it is seldom held in such paradigmatic esteem. It seems in retrospect to have offered few "lessons," either in foreign policymaking circles or policymaking studies in general,[89] even though, arguably, the

Truman Doctrine was the pivotal experience in the Cold War. This neglect might possibly be due to the fact that this was a policy forged by irreplaceable individuals—by Marshalls, Achesons, and Kennans—rather than institutions with corporate memories and ongoing policies. The red-baiting of the State Department in the early 1950s might have effectively driven out of the government whatever continuities that remained. In any event, the events of the Truman Doctrine and the implementing Marshall Plan had little effect on the development of the policy sciences except as an interesting but singular case study in crisis management.

Finally, during the late 1940s and early 1950s, there was a series of major American policy debates and decisions over the development of weapons systems and the services that would be responsible for their operation.[90] Implicit in these debates was the nature and danger of the Soviet threat facing the United States. The issues were recognized at the time as having a major influence on U.S. defense and foreign policies; witness the number of high-level advisory groups counseling President Truman on whether the United States should develop the hydrogen bomb and the pros and cons of the Navy's proposed super carrier.[91] Yet for all the heat (if not light) these controversies generated, they did little to set and anneal the policy sciences. Even within the Department of Defense, the analytic processes which fed the discussions and decisions seemingly had little institutional longevity. The often-cited analytic developments within the Department of Defense (e.g., systems analysis and PPBS) did not appear until the early 1960s with the advent of Robert McNamara's "whiz kids" and their managerial reforms.[92]

The reasons these national security policy controversies and opportunities did not have wide effects on the policy community are matters for conjecture, but two explanations can be offered. First, the deliberations were held predominantly with the Defense Department and the White House, with some involvement from the State Department; there were few chances for outside participation so their external diffusions were minimized. And, second, once the decisions were made, the services devoted all their attention to consolidating their gains or buttressing their positions against possible further incursions by civilian policymakers. The analytic agenda were replaced by administrative items.

TO THE POINT

If these vignettes are fair and representative, they support the observation that some political contexts have had more effect on the policy sciences than other but similar conditions. We thus must ask why some political events have been more conducive to the development of the policy sciences than others. But to do this, we must surrender the separation between the internal and external components of the policy sciences. This marriage has certainly been hinted at. We need now to turn to it directly, a courtship carried out in the next chapter.

ENDNOTES

1. E.g., see Aaron Wildavsky, *The Politics of the Budgetary Process* (Boston: Little, Brown, 1979 ed.).
2. Edith Stokey and Richard Zeckhauser, *A Primer of Policy Analysis* (New York: Norton, 1978); Edward S. Quade, *Analysis for Public Decisions* (New York: Elsevier, 1982), provides examples.
3. Abraham Kaplan, *The Conduct of Inquiry* (San Francisco: Chandler, 1968).
4. This is recognized by Richard C. Larson and Amadeo R. Odoni, *Urban Operations Research* (Englewood Cliffs, NJ: Prentice-Hall, 1981), in their chapter "Implementation."
5. See Garry D. Brewer, *Politicians, Bureaucrats, and the Consultant* (New York: Basic Books, 1973), for an example of the conflict between technique and politics.
6. While this is not explicitly acknowledged, it would appear to be an underlying thesis of Aaron Wildavsky, *Speaking Truth to Power: The Art and Craft of Policy Analysis* (Boston: Little, Brown, 1979).
7. Hardly an easy eask; see Richard E. Neustadt and Ernest R. May, *Lessons in Time* (New York: Free Press, 1986).
8. Alexander L. George, David K. Hall, and William E. Simon, *The Limits of Coercive Diplomacy* (Boston: Little, Brown, 1971).
9. For evidence that this is the usual decisionmaking mode and its unfortunate consequences, see Robert Jervis, *Perception and Misperception in International Politics* (Princeton, NJ: Princeton University Press, 1976).
10. One example of OR applications in the British Bomber Command is found in Freeman Dyson, *Disturbing the Universe* (New York: Harper & Row, 1979). Dyson's recommendations for protecting

RAF bombers, based upon his statistical analyses, were rejected by the command.

11. Robert L. Lineberry, "Policy Analysis, Policy Sciences, and Political Science," paper presented at the American Political Science Association meeting, Chicago, September 1982, p. 7.

12. E.g., Harold D. Lasswell and Abraham Kaplan, *Power and Society* (New Haven: Yale University Press, 1950). This and subsequent examples of the uses of problem-oriented research during World War II are drawn from Eugene M. Lyons, *The Uneasy Partnership* (New York: Russell Sage Foundation, 1969).

13. John Morton Blum, *V was for Victory: Politics and American Culture During World War II* (New York: Harcourt Brace Jovanovich, 1977); the theory is discussed by John Kenneth Galbraith, *A Theory of Price Control* (Cambridge, MA: Harvard University Press, 1950). Galbraith was an OPA administrator.

14. Charles W. Bray, *Psychology and Military Proficiency* (Princeton, NJ: Princeton University Press, 1948). Also see James P. Baxter, *Scientists Against Time* (Boston: Little, Brown, 1946), chap. 25, "Selection and Training."

15. Irvin Steward, *Organizing Scientific Research for War* (Boston: Little, Brown, 1948); and Baxter, *Scientists Against Time*.

16. The most complete account of English intelligence activities and organizations is F. H. Hinsley et al., *British Intelligence in the Second World War*, 3 vols. (London: HMSO: 1979–1984).

17. Lyons, *The Uneasy Partnership*, p. 89.

18. Both the CEA and NSF examples are briefly described by Nelson W. Polsby, *Political Innovation in America* (New Haven: Yale University Press, 1984), in terms of policy innovations.

19. The key document in these debates was the report of the President's scientific adviser, Vannevar Bush, *Science, The Endless Frontier* (Washington, DC: U.S. Government Printing Office, 1945).

20. Bruce L. R. Smith, *The RAND Corporation* (Cambridge, MA: Harvard University Press, 1966).

21. Daniel Lerner and Harold D. Lasswell, eds., *The Policy Sciences* (Stanford, CA: Stanford University Press, 1951).

22. See Harold D. Lasswell, "The Political Science of Science," *American Political Science Review* 50, no. 4 (December 1956): 961–979; and Robert K. Merton, "The Role of Applied Social Sciences in the formation of Policy," *Philosophy of Science* 6, no. 3 (July 1949): 161–181.

23. James T. Patterson, *America's Struggle Against Poverty, 1900–1980* (Cambridge, MA: Harvard University Press, 1981), entitles his chapter on this period "The Rediscovery of Poverty."

24. Most notably, Michael Harrington, *The Other America: Poverty in the United States* (New York: Macmillan, 1963). Twenty-five years later, Harrington looked back on the book and its reverberations, as reported by David E. Robinson, "Celebrating, As It Were, Anniversary on Poverty," *New York Times*, October 7, 1987, p. 24.

25. See Robert A. Levine, *The Poor Ye Need Not Have with You: Lessons from the War on Poverty* (Cambridge, MA: MIT Press, 1970); and Adam Yarmolisky, "The Beginnings of the OEO," in James L. Sundquist, ed., *On Fighting Poverty: Perspectives from Experience* (New York: Basic Books, 1969).
26. The programs are reviewed by Joseph A. Kershaw with Paul N. Cournant, *Government Against Poverty* (Chicago: Markham, for the Brookings Institution, 1970).
27. Richard P. Nathan, "Research Lessons from the Great Society," *Journal of Policy Analysis and Management* 4, no. 3 (Spring 1985): 422.
28. Daniel P. Moynihan, *Maximum Feasible Misunderstanding: Community Action in the War on Poverty* (New York: Free Press, 1969).
29. See Henry J. Aaron, *Politics and the Professors: The Great Society in Perspective* (Washington, DC: Brookings Institution, 1978).
30. Charles Murray, *Losing Ground* (New York: Basic Books, 1984).
31. Patterson, *America's Struggle Against Poverty.*
32. A dawning reflected in the chronologically organized essays of Nathan Glazer, *Ethnic Dilemmas: 1964–1983* (Cambridge, MA: Harvard University Press, 1983).
33. Carol H. Weiss, ed., *Using Social Science Research in Public Policy Making* (Lexington, MA: Heath, 1976); and Charles E. Lindblom and David K. Cohen, *Usable Knowledge: Social Sciences and Social Problem Solving* (New Haven: Yale University Press, 1979), are representative.
34. E.g., Harold D. Lasswell, *A Pre-View of Policy Sciences* (New York: American Elsevier, 1971); and Yehezkel Dror, *Design for Policy Sciences* (New York: American Elsevier, 1971).
35. Yehezkel Dror, "Prolegomena to Policy Sciences," *Policy Sciences* 1, no. 1 (Spring 1970): 138.
36. John Noble Wilford, "New Study Field: Policy Sciences," *New York Times,* August 9, 1970, p. B-16.
37. Aaron, *Politics and the Professors,* details multiple examples of these shortcomings.
38. Murray, *Losing Ground;* and Moynihan, *Maximum Feasible Misunderstanding.*
39. Nathan, "Research Lessons from the Great Society," p. 421.
40. Gene H. Fisher, *Cost Considerations in Systems Analysis* (New York: American Elsevier, 1971); and E. S. Quade, *Systems Analysis and Policy Planning: Applications in Defense* (New York: American Elsevier, 1968).
41. Charles J. Hitch and Roland N. McKean, *The Economics of Defense in the Nuclear Age* (New York: Atheneum, 1965). This and the volumes cited in note 40 were originally RAND Corporation reports.
42. Leslie H. Gelb with Richard K. Betts, *The Irony of Vietnam: The System Worked* (Washington, DC: Brookings Institution, 1979).

43. Compare Colin Gray, "What Has Rand Wrought?" *Foreign Policy*, no. 4 (Fall 1971): 111–129, with Bernard Brodie, "Why Were We So (Strategically) Wrong?" *Foreign Policy*, no. 5 (Winter 1971): 151–161. On a more general basis, see Peter deLeon, "The Influence of Analysis on U.S. Defense Policy," *Policy Sciences* 20, no. 4 (1987): 105–128.

44. All of these are illustrated in Gelb with Betts, *The Irony of Vietnam;* also see note 43 and Neil Sheehan et al., *The Pentagon Papers* (New York: Bantam and the New York Times, 1971).

45. The Watergate period is journalistically described by J. Anthony Lukas, *Nightmare: The Underside of the Nixon Years* (New York: Viking Press, 1976); while the Agnew resignation is covered by Richard M. Cohen and Jules Witcover, *A Heartbeat Away* (New York: Viking Press, 1974).

46. See Michael Johnston, *Political Corruption and Public Policy in America* (Monterey, CA: Cole, 1982), chap. 5; and Peter deLeon, "Public Policy Implications of Systemic Political Corruption," paper presented at the annual meeting of the American Political Science Association, Chicago, 1987.

47. Greenberger and his colleagues identify and review fourteen energy models and analyses; Martin Greenberger et al., *Caught Unawares: The Energy Decade in Retrospect* (Cambridge, MA: Ballinger, 1983).

48. Gary Fromm et al., *Federally Supported Mathematical Models: Survey and Analysis* (Washington, DC: National Science Foundation, 1974); quoted in John P. Weyant, "Quantitative Models in Energy Policy," *Policy Analysis* 6, no. 2 (Spring 1980): 212.

49. Robert Stobaugh and Daniel Yergin, eds., *Energy Futures* (New York: Random House, 1979); Hans Landsberg et al., *Energy: The Next Twenty Years* (Cambridge, MA: Ballinger, for Resources for the Future, 1979), also enjoyed popular sales.

50. Robert W. Tucker, "American Power and the Persian Gulf," *Commentary*, November 1980, pp. 25–41; or Walter J. Levy, "Oil and the Decline of the West," *Foreign Affairs*, Summer 1980, pp. 999–1015.

51. John Bridger Robinson, "Apples and Horned Toads: On the Framework-Determined Nature of the Energy Debate," *Policy Sciences* 15, no. 1 (November 1982): 23–45.

52. Michael Thompson, "Among the Energy Tribes: A Cultural Framework for the Analysis and Design of Energy Policy," *Policy Sciences* 17, no. 3 (November 1984): 336.

53. Aaron Wildavsky and Ellen Tenenbaum, *The Politics of Mistrust* (Beverly Hills, CA: Sage, 1981).

54. See Barry Commoner, *The Politics of Energy* (New York: Knopf, 1979); and Greenberger et al., *Caught Unawares.*

55. Weyant, "Quantitative Models in Energy Policy."

56. P. Brett Hammond, "The Energy Model Muddle," *Policy Sciences* 16, no. 3 (February 1984): 227–243.
57. William Ascher, *Forecasting: An Appraisal for Policymakers and Planners* (Baltimore: Johns Hopkins Press, 1978); and Sergio Koreisha and Robert Stobaugh, "Limits to Models," in Stobaugh and Yergin, eds., *Energy Futures*, appendix.
58. Commoner, *The Politics of Energy*.
59. Eugene Frankel, "Energy and Social Change: An Historian's Perspective," *Policy Sciences* 14, no. 1 (December 1981): 59–73.
60. J. David Roessner, "U.S. Government Solar Policy: Appropriate Roles for Nonfinancial Incentives," *Policy Sciences* 15, no. 1 (November 1982): 3–22, supports this observation with examples from the solar energy industry.
61. Amory B. Lovins, *Soft Energy Paths* (Cambridge, MA: Ballinger, for Friends of the Earth, 1977).
62. Some ideas to this end are presented by Brita Schwarz and John Hoag, "Interpreting Model Results—Examples from an Energy Model," *Policy Sciences* 15, no. 2 (December 1982): 167–181.
63. E.g., Arnold J. Meltsner, "Don't Slight Communication: Some Problems of Analytical Practice," in Giandomenico Majone and Edward S. Quade, eds., *Pitfalls of Analysis* (New York: Wiley, for IIASA, 1980), chap. 8. Charles O. Jones, "If I Only Knew Then . . . ," *Policy Analysis* 5, no. 4 (Fall 1979): 473–479, relates his experience serving on an energy advisory committee.
64. A growing realization; see Mark Crawford, "Back to the Energy Crisis," *Science*, February 6, 1987, pp. 626–627; Robert D. Hershey, Jr., "U.S. Oil Shortages Seem Unavoidable to Many Analysts," *New York Times*, February 17, 1987, pp. 1, 34; and H. D. Saunders, "On the Inevitable Return of Higher Oil Prices," *Energy Policy* 12, no. 3 (September 1984): 310–320.
65. Wildavsky, *Speaking Truth to Power*.
66. Harold D. Lasswell, "The Policy Orientation," in Lerner and Lasswell, eds., *The Policy Sciences*, chap. 1.
67. Compare Yehezkel Dror, "Think Tanks: A New Idea in Government," in Carol H. Weiss and Allen H. Barton, eds., *Making Bureaucracies Work* (Beverly Hills, CA: Sage, 1979); with Martin Bulmer, "Applied Social Research: The Use and Non-Use of Empirical Social Inquiry by British and American Governmental Commissions," *Journal of Public Policy* 1, no. 3 (August 1981): 353–380; and Robert K. Merton, "Social Knowledge and Public Policy," in Aaron Rosenblatt and Thomas F. Giergn, eds., *Social Science and the Practicing Professions* (Cambridge, MA: Abt, 1982).
68. Peter deLeon, "Policy Sciences: The Discipline and the Profession," *Policy Sciences* 13, no. 1 (February 1981): 1–7.
69. Wolfgang Hafele, *Energy in a Finite World: A Global Systems Analysis* (Cambridge, MA: Ballinger, for IIASA, 1981).

70. Bill Keepin, "A Technical Appraisal of the IIASA Energy Scenario," *Policy Sciences* 17, no. 3 (November 1984): 199–275; also see Amory B. Lovins, "Expansion ad absurdum," *Energy Journal* 2, no. 4 (1981): 25–34. In defense of the IIASA energy model, see Wolfgang Hafele and H. H. Rogner, "A Technical Appraisal of the IIASA Energy Scenarios? A Rubuttal," *Policy Sciences* 17, no. 4 (December 1984): 341–366.

71. Harvey A. Averch et al., *How Effective Is Schooling?* (Englewood Cliffs, NJ: Education Technical Publications, 1974).

72. Lineberry, "Policy Analysis, Policy Sciences, and Political Science"; and Edward A. Suchman, *Evaluative Research* (New York: Russell Sage Foundation, 1967).

73. Karl W. Deutsch et al., "Conditions Favoring Advances in Social Science," *Science*, February 5, 1971, pp. 450–459.

74. This theme is developed by Harlan Cleveland, *The Knowledge Executive* (New York: Dutton, 1985).

75. A point well documented by Irving L. Janis, *Groupthink* (Boston: Houghton Mifflin, 1982), regarding Watergate and a number of other political decisions.

76. Daniel Yankelovich and John Doble, "The Public Mood: Nuclear Weapons and the U.S.S.R.," *Foreign Affairs*, Fall 1984, pp. 32–46; and Paul Bracken and Martin Shubek, "Strategic War: What Are the Questions and Who Should Be Asking Them?" *Technology in Society* 4, no. 2 (1982): 155–179.

77. See Albert O. Hirschman, *Exit, Voice, and Loyalty* (Cambridge, MA: Harvard University Press, 1970).

78. Lasswell, "The Policy Orientation," p. 16; also see Harold D. Lasswell and Abraham Kaplan, *Power and Society* (New Haven: Yale University Press, 1950).

79. Charles E. Lindblom, "The Handling of Norms in Policy Analysis," in Paul A. Baran et al., eds., *The Allocation of Economic Resources* (Stanford CA: Stanford University Press, 1959), pp. 160–179; more generally, see Charles E. Lindblom, *The Intelligence of Democracy* (New York: Free Press, 1965).

80. Douglas J. Amy, "Why Policy Analysis and Ethics Are Incompatible," *Journal of Policy Analysis and Management* 3, no. 4 (Summer 1984): 573–591; Douglas Torgerson, "Between Knowledge and Politics: Three Faces of Analysis," *Policy Sciences* 19, no. 1 (July 1986): 33–60; and Frank Fischer, *Politics, Values, and Public Policy: The Problems of Methodology* (Boulder, CO: Westview Press, 1980).

81. Martin Rein, *Social Science and Public Policy* (Baltimore: Penguin, 1976); and Geoffrey Vickers, *Value Systems and Social Process* (New York: Basic Books, 1976).

82. Martin Rein, "Value-Critical Policy Analysis," in Daniel Callahan and Bruce Jennings, eds., *Ethics, Social Sciences, and Policy Analysis* (New York: Plenum, 1983), chap. 5; and Aaron Wildavsky, "The

Once and Future School of Public Policy," *Public Interest*, no. 79 (Spring 1986): 25–41.

83. Abraham Kaplan, *American Ethics and Public Policy* (New York: Oxford University Press, 1963).

84. A point repeatedly documented in Aaron, *Politics and the Professors*, and Ascher, *Forecasting*.

85. Bjorn Wittrock and Peter deLeon, "Policy as a Moving Target: A Call for Conceptual Realism," *Policy Studies Review* 6, no. 1 (August 1986): 44–60.

86. Lasswell, "The Policy Orientation"; and Lyons, *The Uneasy Partnership*.

87. Arthur M. Schlesinger, Jr., *The Coming of the New Deal* (Boston: Houghton Mifflin, 1959).

88. See the authoritative Joseph M. Jones, *The Fifteen Weeks* (New York: Viking Press, 1955); and Dean Acheson, *Present at the Creation* (New York: Norton, 1969).

89. A possible exception is Polsby, *Political Innovation in America*, who uses the episode as one of his eight case studies.

90. See Barton J. Berstein, "Truman and the H-Bomb," *Bulletin of the Atomic Scientists* 40, no. 3 (March 1984): 12–18; Warner R. Schilling et al., *Strategy, Politics, and Defense Budgets* (New York: Columbia University Press, 1962); and Paul Y. Hammond, "Super Carriers and the B-36 Bombers," in Harold Stein, ed., *American Civil-Military Decisions* (Birmingham: University of Alabama Press, 1963).

91. The latter, of course, was little more than a subterfuge as to whether the Air Force or the Navy would have the primary strategic weapons delivery responsibilities and capabilities. See Fred Kaplan, *The Wizards of Armageddon* (New York: Simon & Schuster, 1983).

92. See Kaplan, *Wizards of Armageddon*; and Alain Enthoven and C. Wayne Smith, *How Much Is Enough?* (New York: Harper & Row, 1971).

4 / Advice *and* Consent

If they be two, they are two so
  As stiff twin compasses are two;
Thy soul, the fixed foot, makes no show
  To move, but doth, if th' other do.

And though it in the center sit
  Yet when the other far doth roam,
It leans and harkens after it,
  And grows erect, as that comes home.

—John Donne
"A Valediction: Forbidding Mourning"

The preceding two chapters have mapped out two paths in the development of the policy sciences, which we have called the advice and consent paths. The first dealt with the academic disciplines' contributions to the policy sciences; the second with the political events which encouraged their application and thereby shaped the policy sciences' agenda. For much of this narrative, these were independent actors; fellow travelers were infrequent, coincidental, and fleeting. For the policy sciences to achieve the goals set out by their proponents, however, convergence between the two was necessary. For this reason, a resolution of their often parallel but independent tracks must be proposed.

To do this, we must abandon the heretofore arbitrary but useful distinction between the endogenous and exogenous variables which has been observed in the two prior chapters. The internal and external components of the policy sciences must be meshed if we are to understand the evolution and practice of their approach. As an illustrative metaphor, the economist's supply-demand model is appropriate. In some instances, the analyst's intellectual capabilities (supply) were in stock but the political contexts (demand) were not conducive to their use. To borrow Aaron's depiction, politicians did not recruit professors;[1] in the economist's phrase, "supply did not equal demand." This asymmetry might describe the situation which characterized the New Deal, when policy problems were plentiful and pressing yet there was little evidence of regularized policy research. In other instances, the political opportunities might have been present, but the policy-oriented research community was not (for whatever reason) up to the occasion. Practical applications of social science research were not perceived by policymakers, therefore neither solicited nor supported. Moreover, governments which held to a stance of minimal social involvement had little cause to commission research on social issues. Once again, supply did not equal demand, an imbalance that might have been the case in the periods following World Wars I and II. Advice and consent were less than connubial; whatever unions were consummated proved to be of such a transitory nature that they had little effect on the development of the policy sciences.

It was not until the intellectual developments within the policy sciences were secure enough in terms of both organizational and intellectual resources that they could begin to take advantage of the fledgling opportunities presented by political events and make their capabilities known to policymakers, that is, even to apply for the job. Part of the exercise, of course, was to make their institutionalized (as opposed to individual) presence known. During the Great Depression–New Deal, routinized policy advice was a virtually unknown and surely untested commodity. In contrast, when the War on Poverty was declared, the policy sciences' communities were willing and able to volunteer their services; indeed, they helped write the scenarios (policy innovation), played the leading roles (policy implementation), and scripted the reviews (policy evaluation). Similarly, policy analysts were piece and parcel of Vietnam and the energy crises. In these instances, supply and demand were roughly joined, affirming Wagner and Wollmann's observation that "there is a clear link between the demand on the part of the policy-makers and the administrators for policy-relevant research and the evolution of research responding to such signals and stimuli."[2] This is not to say that they were equal or even well matched to the tasks. The union might have seemed well-thought-out but hardly harmonious. Still, given the intimacy of the analysts and the political contexts, it is not surprising that they substantially affected one another and, as a result, the policy sciences writ large.

This interaction is important to examine, for it would be too glib to argue that there is a forcing partner in this union. Typically, the political situation is characterized as predominant. In some cases, this is unassailably true. The Cold War traumas which produced the Marshall Plan overwhelmed whatever sophisticated research methodologies policy scientists might have brought to Truman's counsels. Nor did McNamara's "rational," detached analysis of Soviet missiles in Cuba sway the day in the Ex Comm's deliberations. More recently, one is struck by the lack of analysis which underlay President Reagan's decision to establish his Strategic Defense Initiative. In a *Newsweek* interview, the President was asked, "When did you first hear of or think about this idea?" His response emphasizes the ascendancy of political disposition relative to analysis:

> It kind of amuses me that everybody is so sure I must have heard about it, that I never thought of it myself. The truth is that I did. . . . At one of my regular meetings with the [Joint] Chiefs of Staff, I brought up this subject about a defensive weapon . . . and I asked them, "Is it possible in our modern technology of today that it would be worthwhile to see if we could not develop a weapon that could perhaps take out, as they left their silos, those nuclear missiles?". . . And when they did not look aghast at the idea and instead said yes, they believed that such a thing offered a possibility and should be researched, I said "Go."[3]

The swine flu panic and its preventative programs under the Ford administration are yet two more examples in which political events superseded policy analysis.[4] The policy process which the Tower Commission reported led to the Iran-Contra debacle is further proof that analysis can still be absent from even the most critical government policies and policymaking circles. The upshot is that political decisions were being made without the best available information. While this condition might not preclude successful policies or specific programs, it would appear to reduce that possibility and—more important—needlessly so because analysis need not preclude a political decision. Rather, it can inform and hence improve both the decision and the decision progress or, in Lasswell's words, "the means by which all who participate in a policy-forming and policy-executing process can live up to their potential for sound judgment."[5]

On the other side of the policy sciences coin, tools and concepts have occasionally dominated the policy research agenda. As Mead has noted, academic theories have influenced important policy debates:

> . . . the intellectual genesis of major recent policy shifts has often occurred outside government. Keynesian, monetarist, and supply-side approaches to economic policy, compensatory education and training programs to combat disadvantage, income maintenance and work incentive approaches to poverty, and the deregulation of several industries (airlines, energy, securities)—for all these innovations, the seminal thinking came from university researchers or think tanks, not policy analysts in government.[6]

Many of these concepts led directly to government policies. For instance, economists' arguments forwarded during the 1960s regarding the inherent economic inefficiencies of governmental regulation in a number of markets (e.g., natural gas and interstate transportation) provided the rationale for the subsequent deregulation movements.[7] Still, there were numerous other cases in which the approach forced the findings and recommendations, where the policy problem was made to conform to the theoretic concept. This was readily apparent during the energy crises, as computer modeling assumed a tyrannical role in shaping the questions asked and the advice rendered. "Rational" analysis was the model repeatedly held up during the Vietnam debates. Cost-benefit and PPBS analyses were carelessly transformed from the RAND-devised Defense Department incarnations to HEW's social programs and affected many policymakers' perceptions of their problems and proposed solutions.[8] Many social welfare studies and education evaluations have fallen prey to the techniques and restraints of regression analyses without recognizing the powerful assumptions these techniques ascribe to a study, or even determining if such tools are appropriate.[9] Whether these method-dictated analyses were successful (and most were decidedly not) is beside the point being made here; what is germane is that there were multiple incidents in which the method—not the context or event—both drove the analysis and restricted the recommendations.

Where and when either of these asymmetric conditions occurred, the policy studies were often relegated to political obscurity or impotence, probably to the comfort of all concerned. The expression of a report "bound on all four sides" is not without meaning and solace.

The point is not that advice and consent cannot exist without each other, but that the two can interact to provide better information to the processes of government. Surely no one need worry whether the various disciplines could continue to evolve in hermetic isolation from their social contexts, as indeed they have; there is no immutable law that academics must display social consciences. Nor should one doubt that political decisions will continue to be made without any knowledge of ordinary least squares or decision trees. For our purposes, it is sufficient to note that the advice and consent paths have intersected, and it is these junctures that have shaped the policy sciences. They provided knowledge both of content and procedure in the policy process and thus molded the ways in which the discipline perceived and treated the world.

This convergence thesis explains why political events such as Vietnam had such an effect on the evolution of the policy sciences while the Korean war—which was just as brutal and controversial—seems to have been less influential in the development of the policy sciences. The former struck a number of resonant chords in the policy sciences' approach, thereby basically affecting how analysts and policymakers viewed and orchestrated the policy process. That many of the experiences were negative (i.e., what not to do) is irrelevant for there were still important "lessons learned." However disheartening the Korean conflict was and although it vitally affected American foreign policy for the rest of the decade, it did not have similar effects on how one "worked the problem," at least partially because the cognitive fields of the policy sciences were not sufficiently tilled nor institutionally staffed to assimilate the experiences of the Korean conflict.

The supply-demand metaphor is complementary—but certainly not identical—to Wildavsky's statement that "analysis of policy . . . always considers resources and objectives, means and ends together, never separately." He defines policy analysis by introducing the expressions "social interaction" and "intellectual cogitation" as its twin lodestones: "Policy analysis . . . is about combining social interaction with intellectual cogitation." And later: "If the reader will allow me my preference for two-thirds politics and one-third planning, this hybrid of social interaction and intellectual cogitation may be called policy analysis."[10] If we can once more equate "intellectual cogitation" with means (supply) and "social interaction" with ends (demand), then we find Dror agreeing that "the interaction between means and ends is most important. Often ends, both operational and general values (though perhaps not final values), change because of innovations in means."[11] Torgerson, with yet another pair, reaches complementary conclusions:

> The dynamic nature of the [policy sciences] phenomenon is rooted in an internal tension, a *dialectical opposition between knowledge and politics*. Through the interplay of knowledge and politics, different aspects of the phenomenon become salient at different moments. . . . The presence of dialectical tension means that the phenomenon has the potential to develop, to change its form. However, no particular pattern of development is inevitable.[12]

Although Wildavsky, Dror, or Torgerson would hardly claim license to speak for the entire policy sciences community, their observations do lend credence to our thesis that the policy sciences are jointly defined by intellectual contributions and political events, that there is no universally correct proportion (Wildavsky's preferred blend not withstanding) for these elements, and that it is the combination of these elements that provides grist for the successful analytic mill. Thus, it is not surprising that those analytic episodes which combined the two have had the greatest influence on the development of the policy sciences.

The supply-demand image, like any metaphor, should not be stretched too far. Still, it does illustrate the point that the evolution of the policy sciences is an integrated function of both internal and external variables, of thought and practice. Requests for advice sown on an intellectually fallow field will probably bear little fruit; methodological wizardries lacking relevant problems are likewise sterile cuttings in the policy sciences' vineyard. The necessary juxtaposition thus suggests why some political events have been far more fruitful to the growth of the policy sciences than others, which leads us to examine more closely the nature of these harmonies. That is, how have these two otherwise independent paths reached some kind of synergistic policy-oriented resolution in some instances and not in others?

WHAT HARMONIES?

One should not aspire to being definitive in answering the question, for the relationship between approaches and events is variable and will change to meet new and perhaps unforeseen contingencies.* There is and should be little that is conclusive in the policy sciences. If the Great Society programs, Vietnam, and the energy crises taught anything to policy scholars and practitioners, it should have been humility regarding both the power of their tools and their roles in actual political decisionmaking. In Bulmer's words:

> If a conclusion is required, let it be one about what social science can hope to contribute to policy. Social science is likely to contribute most by blending its theoretical insights with empirical inquiry, by cultivating the interpretation of the world through a judicious mixture of the concrete and abstract.[13]

Such modest proposals are reciprocated by the perceptions of persons in policymaking positions. Weiss's interviewees could cite few examples in which policy research had made a difference in their policy decisions.[14] Kasschau, in her study of the elderly, found that policymakers drew more upon the "mass media" than "scientific research."[15] Schneider and her colleagues attribute this attitude at least partially to the lack of rigorous (i.e., quantitative) paradigms and methodologies.[16]

On the more positive side, Caplan's study of knowledge utilization by federal executives found that policymakers described

---

*The contrary, distressing, and understandable position of generals preparing to fight the last war is all too familiar.

themselves as quite aware of and responsive to policy research. In direct opposition to Schneider's claims, Caplan and his associates concluded:

> Present knowledge utilization theories are often limited by their over-reliance on an assumed pattern of knowledge use involving "hard" information (i.e., data-based). We found that this type of social science knowledge is used in a vast number of different contexts, that it is used a large number of times, but only rarely is policy formulation determined by a concrete, point-by-point reliance on empirically grounded data. Although the impact of "soft" information (i.e., nonempirical) on government function is extremely difficult to assess, our data suggest that there is widespread use of soft information and that its impact on policy, although often indirect, may be great or even greater than the impact of hard information.

They explained that where a gap existed between policy advisers and policymakers, it was "due to differences in values, language, reward systems and social and professional affiliations. More generally, it suggests that the factors responsible for the gap between the humanities and the hard sciences play a similar role in keeping the social science knowledge producers and knowledge users apart."[17]

While modesty might be warranted, there are dangers to such reticence, to assuming a largely reactive role. For the policy research community to assume the recalcitrant stance of "enlightenment" or "knowledge creep" as its most realistic aspirations would undercut whatever political opportunities might arise.[18] Moreover, such a posture would truncate the continued development of the policy sciences and whatever promise they might hold for better governance.[19] Policy entrepreneurs should not become an endangered species, as was perhaps the case in the mid 1950s. At the same time, one must be careful that supply is not permitted to create its own demand or squander the opportunities that might present themselves. Analysts were unable to fulfill their evaluation promises when they clamored to formulate and then assess the antipoverty program in the late 1960s and early 1970s, thereby raising legitimate questions regarding the value of their product.[20]

The pivotal criterion here is the crucial, ongoing dialogue

within the policy sciences between its internal and external angels. Political events and policy approaches must be in close match or harmony, or at least not be dissonant; both are critical, and neither can be neglected. Political contingencies cannot be ignored but they cannot be allowed to dominate; in Wildavsky's words, "the main task of responsible intellectual cogitation is to monitor, appraise, modify, and otherwise strengthen social interaction."[21] Their harmonies might not be precisely tuned in advance. Neither, however, should either be permitted to proceed unaccompanied by the other if one wishes to understand the development and future of the policy sciences.

The disconnects between the two—that is, when the methodologies do not jibe with the political events and vice versa—have been commonplace. They produced a series of frustrations and disappointments; policy researchers' works were regularly relegated to the shelf of forgotten reports, and the policymakers were rarely left with feasible solutions to their problems. Specific examples are useful here in illustrating how methodological approaches have warped policy analyses and subsequent recommendations. There is strong evidence that the statistical measures and procedures employed by Coleman in his landmark study, *Equality of Educational Opportunity*, were not equal to the tasks at hand and, in fact, fundamentally skewed his findings and rendered any policy recommendations suspect.[22] Housing models have consistently proven to be unable to predict urban land use patterns.[23] We have already seen how energy models and simulations strongly biased the energy debates.[24] Indeed, models in general have proven to be lucrative but largely inadequate policy research devices because of their theory and data deficiencies.[25] There is little need to recount the great number of times in which politics—pure and simple—overrode any analytic contributions to policymaking; the controversies over income supplement plans (in particular negative income taxes) and urban renewal programs are only two of many.

Furthermore, even when supply does seem to match demand, propitious results are far from guaranteed. The analytic track standards recorded during the Vietnam conflict, the War on Poverty, and the energy crises should warn against any unwarranted optimism in this regard. Rather, they highlight the difficulty of the problems—both political and methodological—faced by the policy research communities.

In its barest statement, these observations are little more than having some confidence that effective policy research requires that the internal and external variables are consonant with each other's constraints and capabilities. Otherwise, policy analysis is reduced to the almost-random utility Lindblom and Cohen describe as "professional social inquiry."[26] Indeed, given the occasional tendencies for government intervention to be counterproductive, conditions might become even worse than if they had been left unattended.[27] The recommendation is more than a counsel to try harder, to do better; floundering, regardless of how well intended, rarely works. To revise Kaplan's adage, make sure that you have the proper hammer before hitting the appropriate nail.

To recap briefly: the varying political effects of political events on the policy sciences were less a singular function of their political or institutional magnitudes and more a result of the combination of—the harmony between—their political ramifications and the ability of the policy sciences' paradigms and approaches to accommodate them. The whole was greater than the sum of the parts. Additional examples of these synergistic convergences— such as the Manhattan Project, various environmental crises (e.g., Love Canal), and possibly the "Challenger" disaster—might be explored to substantiate this thesis. Similarly, other political events that have seemingly been less influential (e.g., *Brown* v. *Board of Education*, the continuing series of crisis in education reports, and the urban riots of the mid 1960s) should be investigated to propose amending hypotheses.

The recognition of the "lessons" derived from the political events related above does not necessarily portend more responsive, successful policy sciences; to amend the economist's dictum, there are no cheap lunches. Political contexts may require a multidisciplinary approach, but the accompanying costs should be appreciated and taken into account. To implement the multidisciplinary research mode, one must partially abandon the underlying theories which define the contributing disciplines. In so doing, the analyst loses the use of those paradigms for framing the problem and must rely on more extemporaneous, less documented or tested models. Where or what, the analyst needs to ask, are the policy gaps in, for instance, Keynesian economics or human capital theory? In addition, the boundary conditions—where one discipline blends into another (e.g., political sociology and social psychology)—are gray, amorphous areas. As Simon cautioned many years ago, to disassemble and then reassemble a problem along multidisciplinary perspectives introduces new complexities into an already complicated condition.[28] In many cases, these could be significant sacrifices and should caution against a willy-nilly enlistment on the multidisciplinary bandwagon.

Similar reservations apply to the thoughtless inclusion of normative standards into policy research. That they are important is beyond dispute. What is much more at issue is how their consideration is incorporated in the analytic exercise; the fact that they are not subject to quantitative analysis does not relieve the analyst from conceptual rigor and exposition. Lacking this attention, the normative elements in a policy problem could become entangled in the tired fact-value debate to the benefit of neither the researcher nor the sponsor.[29]

TO CONCLUDE

Before concluding this chapter, it must be made clear that the thesis that disciplinary approaches and political events have both contributed to the development of the policy sciences does not imply in any way that the policy sciences will take precedence over political imperative in policymaking arenas. Political requirements, however loosely and ambiguously defined, will be the cutting edge in decisionmaking because public policy decisions are, at heart, political decisions and, as in all matters of the heart, pure logic, no matter how apparently "correct," must take a back seat.

In summary, we have proposed that external events are more likely to influence the development of the policy sciences if the organizational and cognitive groundwork has been laid. Lacking these prerequisites, political events of such magnitude as the Great Depression, the Marshall Plan, and the Korean conflict failed to flavor the policy sciences' stew as richly as the Great

Society, the energy crises, and the Vietnam war. If this is true, it follows that the class of events should be just as important as the receptors. Thus, it is impossible to say that either the advice or supply path was more influential in laying out the policy science avenues, for it was their intersections that in fact supplied the determining directions.

Therein lies the continuing challenge for the policy sciences: to sharpen their conceptual and organizational tools so that they can accept new assignments with some confidence of success. To these ends, the experiences of World War II, the antipoverty crusade, the Vietnam war, Watergate, and the energy crises were juxtaposed with the disciplinary contributions to provide the conceptual and practical milestones of the policy sciences' approach. These interactions have potentially set the stage for the policy sciences to cope with new emergencies and opportunities. It is to this future that we now turn our attention.

ENDNOTES

1. Henry J. Aaron, *Politics and the Professors: The Great Society in Perspective* (Washington, DC: Brookings Institution, 1978). Aaron was the Assistant Secretary for Planning and Evaluation in the Department of Health, Education, and Welfare during the late 1970s.
2. Peter Wagner and Hellmut Wollmann, "Social Scientists in Policy Research and Consulting: Some Cross-National Comparisons," *International Social Science Journal* 38, no. 4 (1986): 603.
3. Richard M. Smith, "The President's View," *Newsweek*, March 18, 1985, p. 21. The lack of substantive and institutional preparation is also noted by John Newhouse, "The Diplomatic Round: Summiteering," *New Yorker*, September 9, 1986, p. 50.
4. Richard E. Neustadt and Harvey V. Feinberg, *The Epidemic That Never Was* (New York: Vintage Books, 1983); and Arthur M. Silverstein, *Pure Politics and Impure Science: The Swine Flu Affair* (Baltimore: Johns Hopkins Press, 1981). The Neustadt-Feinberg account was commissioned by Joseph Califano, Secretary of Health, Education, and Welfare under President Carter.
5. Harold D. Lasswell, *A Pre-View of Policy Sciences* (New York: American Elsevier, 1971), pp. 62–63.
6. Lawrence M. Mead, "Science versus Analysis: A False Dichot-

omy," *Journal of Policy Analysis and Management* 4, no. 3 (Spring 1985): 421.

7. See John W. Kingdon, *Agendas, Alternatives, and Public Policies* (Boston: Little, Brown, 1983). For a recent assessment of these arguments and their results, see the articles on regulatory reforms in the *Journal of Policy Analysis and Management* 5, no. 3 (Spring 1986): 440–534.

8. George W. Downs and Patrick Larkey, *The Search for Government Efficiency* (New York: Random House, 1986), chaps. 4 and 5.

9. From a philosophical perspective, see William Barrett, *The Illusions of Technique* (New York: Doubleday, 1978); Garry D. Brewer and Peter deLeon, *The Foundations of Policy Analysis* (Homewood, IL: Dorsey, 1983), part 2, "Estimation," talk to these problems in more concrete terms. Also see Henry Acland, "Are Random Experiments the Cadillac of Design?" *Policy Analysis* 5, no. 3 (Spring 1979): 223–242.

10. Aaron Wildavsky, *Speaking Truth to Power: The Art and Craft of Policy Analysis* (Boston: Little, Brown, 1979), pp. 10, 12, and 124.

11. Yehezkel Dror, *Public Policymaking Reexamined* (San Francisco: Chandler, 1968), p. 16.

12. Douglas Torgerson, "Between Knowledge and Politics: Three Faces of Policy Analysis," *Policy Sciences* 19, no. 1 (1986): 52, fn. 4; emphases in original.

13. Martin Bulmer, *The Uses of Social Research* (London: George Allen & Unwin, 1982), p. 166.

14. Carol H. Weiss, ed., *Using Social Research in Public Policy* (Lexington, MA: Heath, 1977).

15. Patricia L. Kasschau, *Aging and Social Policy* (New York: Praeger, 1978).

16. Janet A. Schneider et al., "Policy Research and Analysis: An Empirical Profile, 1975–1980," *Policy Sciences* 15, no. 2 (December 1982): 99–114. Ronald D. Brunner, "The Policy Sciences as Science," *Policy Sciences* 15, no. 2 (December 1982): 115–136, contests the Schneider interpretation.

17. Nathan Caplan et al., *The Use of Social Science Knowledge in Policy Decisions at the National Level* (Ann Arbor: Institute for Social Research, University of Michigan, 1975), pp. 47 and 27, respectively.

18. As posed by, *inter alia*, Carol H. Weiss, *Social Science Research and Decision Making* (New York: Columbia University Press, 1980).

19. See Bjorn Wittrock, "Governance in Crisis and Withering of the Welfare State: The Legacy of the Policy Sciences," *Policy Sciences* 15, no. 3 (April 1983): 195–204.

20. Martin Rein and Sheldon H. White, "Can Policy Research Help Policy?" *Public Interest*, no. 49 (Fall 1979): 119–136. Robert Scott and Arnold Shore, *Why Sociology Does Not Apply: A Study of the*

Use of Sociology in Public Policy (New York: Elsevier, 1979), examine this concern from a disciplinary standpoint; more generally, see Charles E. Lindblom and David K. Cohen, *Usable Knowledge* (New Haven: Yale University Press, 1979).

21. Wildavsky, *Speaking Truth to Power*, p. 12.

22. Frederick Mosteller and Daniel P. Moynihan, eds., *On Equality of Educational Opportunity* (New York: Random House, 1972); also see Aaron, *Politics and the Professors*, chap. 3.

23. Garry D. Brewer, *Politicians, Bureaucrats, and the Consultant* (New York: Basic Books, 1973); and Garry D. Brewer and Owen P. Hall, Jr., "Policy Analysis by Computer Simulation: A Need for Appraisal," *Public Policy* 21, no. 3 (Summer 1973): 343–365.

24. Martin Greenberger et al., *Caught Unawares: The Energy Decade in Retrospect* (Cambridge, MA: Ballinger, 1983).

25. William Ascher, *Forecasting: An Appraisal for Policymakers and Planners* (Baltimore: Johns Hopkins University Press, 1978); Holcomb Research Institute, *Environmental Modeling and Decision Making* (New York: Praeger, 1976); and Robert F. McNown, "On the Uses of Econometric Models: A Guide for Policymakers," *Policy Sciences* 19, no. 4 (1986): 359–380.

26. Lindblom and Cohen, *Usable Knowledge.*

27. For examples in the field of welfare reforms, see Nathan Glazer, *Ethnic Dilemmas: 1964–1983* (Cambridge, MA: Harvard University Press, 1983); and Charles Murray, *Losing Ground* (New York: Basic Books, 1984). The counterargument—that things would have been much worse without the Great Society Programs—is made by John E. Schwarz, *America's Hidden Success* (New York: Norton, 1983).

28. Herbert A. Simon. "The Architecture of Complexity," *General Systems Yearbook*, vol. 10 (1965); and Herbert A. Simon, *The Sciences of the Artificial* (Cambridge, MA: MIT Press, 1969).

29. Martin Rein, *Social Sciences and Public Policy* (Baltimore: Penguin, 1976), chap. 2, "The Fact-Value Dilemma"; Frank Fischer, *Politics, Values, and Public Policy: The Problem of Methodology* (Boulder, CO: Westview Press, 1980), chap. 2, "The Fact-Value Debate and the Search for Methodology"; and Frank Fischer and John Forester, eds., *Confronting Values in Policy Analysis* (Newbury Park, CA: Sage, 1987).

5 / The Future of the Policy Sciences

Surgeons must be very careful
When they take the knife.
Underneath their fine incisions
Stirs the culprit, life.

—Emily Dickinson
"Surgeons Must Be Very Careful"

DON'T ASK HARD QUESTIONS . . .

The previous chapters have traced the development of the policy sciences as a twin function of intellectual and contextual events. We have seen how these have influenced the policy sciences, in terms of both their concepts and practices and their partial effect on how political events were perceived and treated. We need now to turn to a final task, a discussion of the future of the policy sciences given this dual heritage. An up-front caveat: this exercise will be even more idiosyncratic than the expositions of the earlier chapters. Those chapters are more or less descriptive, offering perceived trends and references from the illustrative grab bag of history, with only an occasional interpretative aside to argue for a certain thesis or theme. This chapter is deliberately more speculative. It very much reflects my vision of what is currently remiss with the policy sciences, how these shortcomings might be remedied, and, most holistically, what the continuing development of the policy sciences should resemble.

This last item is particularly important, for there are two possible developmental paths, both of which must admit to the serendipity of future events. The first, one resembling a natural evolution, surrenders the policy sciences to the relatively random eddies of its component internal and external variables. An intellectual cachet may capture analysts' attention, such as was the case with cost-benefit and PPBS analyses during the 1960s, and then fade into oblivion. Political events may impact the approach, as was the case in the energy crises. Lastly, political institutions and ideologies may play a key role; for instance, it is widely believed that the Reagan administration has not been particularly receptive to policy research, especially that which does not pass its ideological litmus tests,[1] even when it comes from within its own ranks.[2] In short, stochastic processes—Machiavelli referred to them more poetically as *virtu*—may play the dominant role in determining the future of the policy sciences.[3] The second path is much more deterministic and holds that policy scientists themselves can assume an instrumental role in the future of their profession, in terms of both the approaches they employ and the policy problems they address. These choices, of course, will not always be readily available, but neither will they be beyond their control.

Not surprisingly, the appropriate road would seem to fall somewhere between these two avenues. It implies that unpredictable policy events will occur and have a critical effect on the development of the policy sciences, but that the policy sciences can be prepared for these unforeseen emergencies or, more positively, opportunities. The Red Cross cannot safely predict and plan for every conceivable disaster, but it does have contingency plans in hand to handle most floods, fires, and other catastrophes without having to resort to "worst case" analysis. Similarly, the policy sciences need not aspire to being the universal solvent; too often, such elixirs turn out to be snake oils. "The theory of second best informs economists that if one or more conditions necessary for a maximum are not present—which is the way of the world—there often is no way of telling where [or what] a second best solution would be."[4] The ability to advise on most of the problems most of the time should be a sufficient goal. This stands in contrast to a recent professional failing, the willingness to issue promissory notes on all of the problems all of the time, a "beltway bandit" mentality which predictably contributed to everybody's embarrassment and disillusion. A Nobel laureate physicist once claimed that he had never seen a policy problem he could not solve over a weekend. There is little reason to suppose that he—let alone the quotidian analyst—could so charm the policy marketplace as a workaday event.

Before proceeding, we need to admit to a central paradox between policy advice and policy consent, one which presents a troublesome dilemma. On the one hand, the policy advice industry is, by any number of standards, growing in size and respectability. Virtually every university features a graduate program in public policy analysis and administration whose sole function— however unevenly performed—is to stock the profession with accredited analysts. It is a rare government agency or department that does not have its own designated analysis unit, an observation certainly true on the federal level and increasingly true within the states and most large municipalities. The number of consultant firms and individuals continues to grow in spite of the cutbacks of the Reagan administration and state budget restrictions (e.g., California's Proposition 13); one would like to hope that good policy research is even more critical during times of austerity (i.e., what should be cut?) than prosperity.[5] It would be almost impossible to estimate accurately the amounts of money spent on analytic exercises for any given year. Accounting identities befuddle any "guesstimate": the inclusion or exclusion of internal (i.e., staff) and external (consultant) fundings (full or part time?) and at what levels (federal, state, local) and what sources (just government and not foundation funding?) would make such a calculation little better than hypothetical.[6] Still, it is safe to say that hundreds of millions, probably billions, of dollars fuel the supply side of the policy sciences expression. In short, as the accountants among us show, somebody is willing to pay richly for professional policy study and analysis because the advice/supply side of the policy sciences ledger is poshly funded—which, from a standpoint of the aggregate "industry," is well and good.

On the other hand, while the demand for institutionalized policy research and advice has never been greater, most realistic analysts recognize—however reluctantly—that the value of their product is usually marginal, rarely decisive, and occasionally completely neglected. Politics will dominate analysis. Period. Weiss's review of policymakers' utilizations of social science policy research supports this perception; policymakers typically look to the social sciences in terms of "enlightenment" and "knowledge creep," not concrete policy recommendations, in answer to their immediate problem.[7] Nor is hers an isolated finding; the implementation and evaluation literatures are populated by horror rather than success stories. Hence, the paradox: if this is the case—if policy research seldom answers the policymaker's most insistent mail—why is policy analysis characterized as a "growth industry"? What drives the apparent demand? Who needs it and why? An economist would be hard put to explain why policymakers are willing to spend significant resources for a commodity they hardly use.

The resolution of the posed paradox is far from academic or unimportant, for it affects the very essence of the policy sciences and their founding charter. Therein lies the dilemma. If the policy sciences are to conform to Lasswell's initial vision—one of providing relatively unbiased knowledge both in and of the policy process in matters of great social importance—then the reluctance of the policymaker to accept advice conforming to these standards and the ingratiating willingness of many policy analysts to accept such restrictions violates the basic relevance and rigor tenets of the approach. Policy research would be sponsored if it substantiates predetermined positions or incrementally improves a preferred program. Support rather than information would be its specified product. No wonder, then, when Aaron writes that policy research, "insofar as it exercises independent influences on opinions about complex social questions, tends over time to be profoundly conservative in its impact,"[8] an incremental approach that seeks only to nudge (as opposed to shape) policy programs.

If one adopts this reasonable and surely supportable perspective, then one must accept its crucial implications for the development of the policy sciences. It suggests that the discipline and profession would be lashed to adjustments on the margins, to perfecting what tools they have at their present or near-time disposal. To be fair, these are not trivial charges nor tasks best left for the tyro. Means of incorporating values or cultural distinctions into curricula and even actual analyses will not only occupy the profession's intellectual facilities for years to come, but will also result in a "better" product.[9] This perspective binds one to what Horowitz and Katz once described as the "handmaiden approach" to policy research.[10] Quite legitimately, utility would be the professional hallmark, relevance would reign, and rigor could be a neglected—perhaps conveniently forgotten—way station. It would effectively eliminate the innovative and radical policy recommendations.

However understandable, this view represents a lamentable posture. The policymaking floor might be immaculately painted, but the policy sciences' discipline would find itself in a conceptual corner. As Anderson points out, many major policy decisions were hardly incremental in nature, especially those of a crisis (e.g., the Truman Doctrine) or particularly large start-up (e.g., the Apollo project) character.[11] As was argued earlier, the policy research community was not able to weather the demands showered on it by the War on Poverty or the energy crises. Even Lindblom, the most cited advocate of incremental adjustment and "muddling through," now worries that this perspective would be unduly restrictive in terms of limiting policymakers to simply feasible solutions in lieu of the breathtaking.[12] If true, then the policy sciences should not aspire to being meekly reactive. Political events of the past few decades should make one reluctant to abandon the quantum option. Furthermore, to do so would relegate the policy sciences to a set of ultimately menial, uninteresting exercises.

Without losing sight of the methodological trees (with their cultivations, prunings, and harvestings), this discussion of the future of the policy sciences' development focuses on the forest. Less metaphorically, the chapter proposes some cognitive and intellectual developments which will prepare the policy sciences for the somewhat unpredictable future political contexts in which they must operate.

This does not mean that the future of the policy sciences should neglect the development of their various tools; risk analysis, technology assessment, value-critical analysis, forensic analysis, and other methodologies all warrant continued annealing in the policy research crucibles.[13] Lasswell's developmental construct continues to hold great promise as a comprehensive analytic approach.[14] The establishment of a professional code of conduct would be a welcome—albeit loudly contentious—circumstance. The area of social experiments—their structure, ethical implications, and use—merits close attention.[15] New models of the policy process (at both the micro and macro levels) must be advanced.[16] Hopefully, most of the semantic bickering which confused (and at times amused) neutral observers is now history, although one cannot be sure. Lasswell and Kaplan wrote in 1950:

> [U]niformity of usage cannot be brought about by either fiat or exhortation. Nor is . . . uniformity of any transcending importance. What does matter is self-consistency, and sufficient clarity to make translation and empirical reference always possible. Our concern . . . is not with words but with concepts.[17]

What they wrote is mirrored in Ascher's 1987 editorial under the heading "What Is Now *Passé.*"

> We also need no further exercises in *naming* the various facets of the policy process, if that new nomenclature is simply an equivalent language map of existing vocabularies. This does not reflect any slavish adherence to the Lasswellian vocabulary, but rather a belief that various sound vocabularies exist, and can be improved upon only by introducing new concepts rather than by relabeling the old ones.[18]

Moreover, these preclusions are not meant to downgrade the importance of the innovative application of existing methodologies[19] or the proposal of new approaches to the art and craft, such as the manipulation of political symbols.[20] Canute was as likely able to hold back the waves as a monograph could restrict intellectual and practical growths and innovations. Whatever: the focus of the following is on possible major adaptations in the evolution of the policy sciences, drawing upon what Lasswell called "developmental constructs" (defined as "aids in the total task of clarifying goals, noting trends, and estimating future possibilities").[21]

This emphasis obligates the policy sciences communities to admit frankly that there are certain contexts in which it would be highly plausible that they could generate much heat while providing only scattered light. The issue of abortion and the related one of surrogate parenthood would seemingly defy most forms of logical, rational analysis, although the normative lens of the policy sciences might offer some insights.

Time frames are also key: the further one projects into the future, the more speculative one must be. Even when requirements are quite definite, time has a way of invalidating most "needs" as originally specified. The dire predictions of Malthus evaporated before the winds of the industrial and agricultural revolutions. Similarly, the confident petroleum economies of the industrialized nations were shattered by the energy crises of the 1970s. Resources are equally capricious. In 1980, a Swedish study commission on the long-term availability of natural resources observed:

A few years ago the head of the National Swedish Forest Service was able to report that the oak trunks designated for the construction of [naval] men-of-war were now ready for delivery. The *Riksdag* had earmarked about 25000 acres of land for this purpose in 1829. This rather off-beat example confirms the general rule that a resource does not become a resource until it is related to a certain kind of use in human society.[22]

If we are honest, we must back fumblingly into the future, more secure in what we do not know than what we do.[23] Choosing futures is not a confident option, but preparing for them might be.

Having thus registered sufficient reservations to disavow with dispatch and dispassion what follows, let me now discuss what I think will be key milestones in the future development of the policy sciences if they are to achieve the pomp and circumstance envisioned by their proponents.

. . . UNLESS YOU WANT HARD ANSWERS

In many senses, the future of the policy sciences would seem secure, perhaps even bright. Certainly in comparison to earlier periods, their intellectual and institutional blues seem far behind. As noted above, there is almost an embarrassingly large demand for their services, they are organizationally well ensconced, and they possess a wealth of applicable methodologies. The advice and consent stars are apparently well aligned in the policy sciences constellation, a seeming harmonic convergence. But this smug reading could easily be illusionary, more façade than foundation. University policy programs still continue to be oriented in

terms of disciplines, and therefore are more Quonset huts than
cozy homes for interdisciplinary, policy-directed research scholars
and training.[24] The general demise of university programs in
public administration gives evidence to the mutability of academic
fancies. There are numerous divisive internal debates within the
policy sciences which could prove centrifugal. The financial hard-
ships visited upon the Urban Institute and Mathematica by the
Reagan administration demonstrates that even the most presti-
gious of the "think tanks" are no more safe havens for independent thinking than the medieval churches.[25] And there is scant
evidence that the utilization quandaries posed by Weiss and
others have been settled in favor of policy research. The policy
sciences will continue to be required to answer the oldest and
most insistent of political questions: What have you done for me
lately? And what can you do for me tomorrow?

The answers to these questions are not easy for they imply the
recognition and correction of past shortcomings, both conceptual
and operational. In this area, it suggests an acceptance of what
some observers refer to as the "post-positivist" phase of the policy
scientific inquiry and technology. In Torgerson's description, they
describing and prescribing social interactions.[26] The confidences
engendered by positivism made a distinct impression on many of
the early and subsequent policy scientists; human interactions
could be observed, dissected, and manipulated by the tenets of
scientific inquiry and technology. In Torgerson's description, they
averred that "knowledge would replace politics," especially in the
increasingly technology-oriented world. He continues:

> Consider the conventional posture of the policy analyst. The guid-
> ing outlook is a technocratic one—that is, one of detachment in
> developing knowledge *of* society in order that the knowledge can
> subsequently be applied *to* society. The place of the analyst *in*
> society as a social being dealing with others of his kind tends not to
> be raised as a point of discussion. Removed from society, social
> science produces the knowledge from which to fashion an effective
> social technology; and the analyst—as both scientist and techni-
> cian—becomes one who performs remote operations on an essen-
> tially alien object.

Torgerson concludes that even today, "one gets the feeling that
the professional policy analyst is not really of this world—this all-

too-human world of conflict, confusion, and doubt."[27] As Brunner summarizes, "Positivism is a dead issue among philosophers and historians of science, but it continues to be influential in the behavioral sciences. The aspirations and methods of positivism . . . divert attention from results, which are contingent upon the analyst's selective construction of the context and therefore are limited as a basis for rational or objective decisions."[28]

The seed and germination of the transition from hubris to humility are not hard to track. Lasswell's criticism of strict behavioralism and insistence on political contextuality were initial although largely unheeded reservations. Lasswell and Kaplan's explicit inclusion of political ideology as central components of *Power and Society* was another. Drawing upon Wittgenstein and Heidegger, Barrett warned:

> The lesson of Wittgenstein's career for us lies in the failure of logic to determine a philosophy. . . . At a certain point formal logic has to give way to the more haphazard insights of common sense. The insistence upon exactness has to bow to the requirements of adequacy.

> "The essence of technology is danger," says Heidegger. . . . [T]he danger Heidegger has in mind . . . is that technology, when it becomes total, lifts mankind to a level where it confronts problems with which technical thinking is not prepared to cope.[29]

These precautions were largely swept aside by the fervored blush of behavioralism, economics, and system analysis with their methodological enthusiasms.[30] It was not until the chastening revelations of the 1960s and 1970s—when policy analysts could not untie or even hack the Gordian knots of the decades' major political crises—that the influence of and techniques extolled by the positivist philosophy and the faith in rationality and technology began to show their vulnerable sides.[31]

The positivist influence produced a relatively inflexible structure, one unable to accommodate the maelstroms of political experiences and requirements. Moreover, the policy communities became rather inbred: policy analysts talked only to policymakers. To surmount these conditions requires almost a new paradigm, a post-positivist perspective in which the principal components are twofold: the reaffirmation of the "human" aspects of policy and an expanded set of participants. In combination, the two serve to make the policy sciences more adaptive and responsive to the needs of society at large.

The first requires the open admission that human values pervade the analytic exercise, or what Schon refers to as "reflective practice."

> The idea of reflective practice leads . . . us to recognize that . . . special knowledge is embedded in evaluative frames which bear the stamp of human values and interests. It also leads us to recognize that the scope of technical expertise is limited by situations of uncertainty, instability, uniqueness, and conflict. . . . Whenever a professional claims to "know," in the sense of the technical expert, he imposes his categories, theories, and techniques on the situation.[32]

Values and ideologies—both personal and societal—are already an integral though sub rosa part of the policy sciences, hidden behind the comfortable skirts of objectivity. As Rein explains, "Knowledge becomes partisan in the policy struggle from which it presumes to detach itself."[33] The charge would be for values to be as openly a component of policy analysis as marginal costing and statistical significance are of economic and statistical analysis. The questions then are: What are the relevant set of values, and how best can they be incorporated into the policy process?[34]

This leads us to the second half of the post-positivist expression, an enlargement of the actors ("stakeholders") involved in the policy process or, put succinctly, a more participatory policy sciences. Lindblom sets out the mandate clearly: "Instead of serving the needs of officials alone, help for the ordinary citizen,"[35] because, in point of fact, they—not the assistant secretaries for analysis and evaluation—are the final consumer, the people who stand to gain or lose the most from the implemented programs.

There are theoretical and practical precedents exemplifying these objectives. The work of Habermas focuses on clear communications among participants ("practical discourse" and "communicative competence") to enhance their capabilities and responsibilities, from both a personal and a societal perspective.[36] A practical application was the work of the Berger Commission.[37] Berger, a Canadian jurist, in order to assess the "social, environmental and economic impact regionally" of a trans-Canadian natural gas pipeline, encouraged public hearings from the affected Indian communities which would have otherwise been effectively disenfranchised. The open hearings were conducted in the native languages and local townships. As he later explained:

> No academic treatise or discussion, formal presentation of the claims of native people by the native organizations and their leaders, could offer as compelling and vivid a picture of the goals and aspirations of native people as their own testimony. In no other way could we have discovered the depth of feeling regarding past wrongs and future hopes, and the determination of native people to assert their collective identity today and in the years to come.[38]

The criterion of a more participatory policy process has already been accepted in environmental impact statements; the Berger Commission simply extended it beyond its normal purview. A second example is the 1977 hearings held over the proposed nuclear fuel recycling facility to be built at Windscale, England.[39] Shubik and Bracken raise similar questions regarding expanded public participation in arms control issues, topics heretofore reserved almost exclusively for a very small number of experts and policymakers.[40]

Participatory analysis, however laudable it might sound, is not without its drawbacks. Clear communications or statements of objectives are not always beneficial; indeed, in the conflictual world of interest group politics, they might be counterproductive to effective policy formulation and implementation. As Rein observes, "Ambiguity seems to be essential for agreement."[41] From an operational standpoint, it is highly resource intensive, especially in terms of time. Environmental impact statements can take years to prepare and more years to litigate, adding immensely to the cost of a project and diminishing the credibility of the process. There are any number of policy issues that could not afford the time necessary to permit all interested parties to voice their concern. From a more procedural standpoint, there is the problem of how one assesses the disparate evidence. Majone, favoring a more judicial than analytic model, contends, "The supreme analytic achievement is no longer the computations of optimal strategies, but the design of procedural rules and social mechanisms for the assessment of incomplete and often contradictory evidence."[42] The energy and environmental billingsgates are vivid witnesses to this shortfall, which Majone does little to resolve.

The implication is subtle but unmistakably important. A judicial analytic model, one characterized by the adversary process and cross-examination, would rekindle the long-smoldering debates as to the proper role of policy analysts: Are they detached, relatively objective analysts or are they involved, vested advocates? Of course, in practice the either/or positions are not as distinct as portrayed; the nominal former is often usurped, however discreetly, by the latter. Still, an open airing of the question cannot be deftly dodged. Moreover, one has to inquire as to the equity of the process. Certainly the inequities of the judicial system indicate that this model might put some participants at a severe disadvantage. An adherence to the participatory policy model would insist that the policy sciences must frontally address these dilemmas.

As the policy sciences expand their clientele, they must also be ready to accept new disciplinary practitioners and approaches because the problems that could confront them might easily come from outside their standard ken and practiced tools. Lasswell and Brewer, among others, have warned that tomorrow's crucial public policy issues may well emerge from outside today's comfortable set.[43] Toffler cautioned almost twenty years ago of a "future shock" situation in which baneful events would cascade faster than individuals or governments could handle them.[44] Environmental disasters, such as Chernobyl, Bhopal, and potentially Three Mile Island, imply that the individual or even collective talents of economists, political scientists, and lawyers are not a sufficient base for treating this emerging brand of problems. By the same token, it is clear that "technical problems" cannot be left to the sole discretion of technicians. Technology assessments, however carefully couched, are fundamentally political acts and fall beyond the technical training of engineers and chemists. Genetic engineering and life-extending medical technologies are prime examples of subjects coming to the public forum that have such a bewildering number of facets—technical, institutional, social, environmental, biological, ethical, and economic—that the very idea of a closed group of professionals (call it a study commission) analyzing their operations and implications would be either irresponsible or ludicrous, if not both. The exploration of space might be similarly bewildering.

Crises, almost by definition, are unpredictable and unavoidable, lest they not be crises. To predict with assurance what these crises might be would be an act of baseless and maybe counterproductive speculation; witness the swine flu folly. However, from the perspective of the policy sciences and society at large, it would be even more foolhardy not to assemble a set of intellectual and conceptual tools that would permit policy researchers to be somewhat prepared when the next crisis (or opportunity) presents itself, to confront what Offe calls the inevitable "crises of crisis management."[45] Likewise, institutions, which are consciously designed to restrict surprises, would be smartly advised to develop a more flexible attitude if they are to meet these challenges.[46] Faced with the certain uncertainties of future events, the policy sciences must assemble all the arms they can cognitively and organizationally muster. Forewarned, hence forearmed, is not an available option in this case.

Again, this recommendation, however sensible, is far from straightforward. If the policy sciences aspire to encompass everything, they threaten to cover nothing. Can any discipline *qua* discipline have such amorphous boundaries that it could include such disparate approaches as petroleum engineering and psychiatry and still remain cohesive? What will be the disciplinary pecking order? What about the problems of information overload? Can the physical scientists adapt a more contextual, uncontrolled set of circumstances? The answers are positive, although not securely so. The linchpin is the existence and acceptance of a coherent philosophy of purpose. This history of the policy sciences implies that such a conceptual core does exist, latently if not blatantly. The future vitality of the policy sciences might well depend upon the variegated contributors being able to accept that core and define their contributions accordingly.

AN EPILOGUE

Pulitzer Prize–winning historian Barbara Tuchman minces few words in her condemnation of governing:

> A phenomenon noticeable throughout history regardless of place or period is the pursuit by governments of policies contrary to their own interests. Mankind, it seems, makes a poorer performance of government than of almost any other human activity. In this sphere, wisdom, which may be defined as the exercise of judgment acting on experience, common sense and available information, is less operative and more frustrated than it should be. . . . Why does intelligent mental process seem so often not to function?[47]

Without mounting a point-to-point match with Tuchman's generalization and chosen examples, we have offered a partial answer to her closing question, that the intellectual tools were not always commensurate with the exigencies imposed by political events. This does not imply that if the policy advisers had been up to standards, their advice would have been heeded; to use Tuchman's examples, Troy would not have accepted the Greek horse, George III would not have lost the American colonies, or the excesses of Pope Leo X would not have contributed to the Reformation.

Tuchman's assessment of the policy process is much too harsh. Historians benefit from the retrospective advantage no policymaker can ever enjoy; as Hegel relates, Minerva's owl begins its flight at twilight. More pertinently for our purposes, she ignores the most obvious of possible explanations: if "mankind . . . makes a poorer performance of government than of almost any other human activity," the reason might well be that mankind has no more difficult task nor taxing responsibility. Plainly put, governance is not a push. There is no inherent reason to assume that the helter-skelter of public policymaking should be a matter of intelligent course or the political process produce successful policies and programs as automatically as is reputed to be the case in the private sector.[48] Even if we grant the application of great wisdom, compassion, and efficiencies (surely monumental assumptions) and a lack of self-interest, venality, and numerous other human foibles, governing—steering among the Scylla and Charybdis of legitimately contending stakeholders and gatekeepers—would be a daunting exercise, one fraught with wreckages of even the best-intended voyages. Odysseus had a Caribbean leisure cruise compared with contemporary policy argonauts. Today's "Golden Fleece" (with now-retired Senator Proxmire as its guardian) is a prize to be avoided, not heroically quested.

One should not practically aspire to perfect government, whatever that means; "perfect" defined by one group might be "disaster" for another, as illustrated by the policy gap between the pro-life and pro-choice camps.* Similarly, the philosopher-king, rational actor model of government which the positivist school of thought sought to advance and implement, is equally unobtainable in the hurly-burly circus of politics. As Simon has repeatedly argued, "A theory of rationality that does not give an account of problem solving in the face of complexity is sadly incomplete. It is worse than incomplete: it can be seriously misleading by providing 'solutions' to economic questions that are without operational significance."[49] Again, politics will ultimately dominate analysis.

This does not mean that the policy sciences are at root sterile exercises with little meaning and less effect. If properly prepared, they can serve two extremely valuable functions and, in so doing, begin to fulfill the expectations of their original proponents. First, they can intelligently and routinely *inform* the policymaking process, both in terms of knowledge in (or content) and knowledge of (procedure). New perspectives on old problems and early indications of new ones can be surfaced by the rigorous applications of the policy sciences. In combination, these serve to expand the menu of policy options applicable to social problems. Rein suggests that policy "research evidence does help to make an assault on older, widely held paradigms and that these new findings make it harder to interpret knowledge in the accepted way and also contribute to the development of new paradigms."[50] Second, through their emphasis on values, they can illuminate the role of values in the policymaking process. Values will still be—and ought to be—central to the political exercise. The post-positivist policy sciences would not disturb that relationship. Rather, they would transform the Eastonian "black box" of political decision-making into a more transparent "glass box" in which decisions could be openly viewed and understood, if not always influenced.

Both contributions would surely benefit the body politic in terms of its operations and its general credibility. But neither is feasible unless there is an acceptance of Dickinson's counsel to

---

*Which also illustrates that the art of political euphemism is still thriving.

surgeons, that underneath all the bells and whistles, the posturings and pieties, is a profound appreciation of and respect for human dignity and all that it implies for the personal and public weal. Fortunately, that is a worthwhile and obtainable Grail.

ENDNOTES

1. Irving Louis Horowitz, "Social Science and the Reagan Administration," *Journal of Policy Analysis and Management* 1, no. 1 (Fall 1981): 126–129; a more recent and general assessment is Lester M. Salamon and Michael S. Lund, eds., *The Reagan Presidency and the Governing of America* (Washington, DC: Urban Institute, 1984).
2. The inability of analysis to inform, let alone determine, the economic policies of the Reagan administration is chronicled by one of the administration's earliest "true believers," David Stockman, *The Triumph of Politics* (New York: Harper & Row, 1985).
3. Herbert Kaufman, *Time, Change, and Organizations* Chatham, NJ: Chatham House, 1985), argues that natural forces, i.e., those beyond institutional control, are the determining factors in organizational life spans.
4. John E. Brendel, "Distilling Frenzy from Academic Scribbling: How Economics Influences Politicians," *Journal of Policy Analysis and Management* 4, no. 3 (Spring 1985): 352.
5. New York City commissioners made just such a claim when describing the impact of New York City's financial crisis upon their individual departments; see Demetrios Caralay, *Doing More with Less* (New York: Graduate Program in Public Policy and Administration, Columbia University, 1982).
6. Drawing upon National Science Foundation documents, John E. Koehler, "The Study, Analysis, and Advice Industry" (Santa Monica, CA: RAND Corporation, P-5433, May 1975), estimated a federal budget expenditure on policy-oriented research of $2.1 billion for 1970. There is no reason to assume that this figure has diminished, even if expressed in constant dollars.
7. Carol H. Weiss, *Social Science and Political Decision Making* (New York: Columbia University Press, 1980).
8. Henry J. Aaron, *Politics and the Professors: The Great Society in Perspective* (Washington, DC: Brookings Institution, 1978), p. 17.
9. Subjects respectively addressed by Martin Rein, *Social Science and Public Policy* (Baltimore: Penguin, 1976), and Aaron Wildavsky, "The Once and Future School of Public Policy," *Public Interest*, no. 79 (Spring 1986): 25–41.

10. Irving Horowitz and James Katz, *Social Science and Public Policy in the United States* (New York: Praeger, 1975), pp. 156–157.
11. James E. Anderson, *Public Policy-Making* (New York: Holt, Rinehart, & Winston, 1984 ed.), p. 10. For a more targeted discussion, see Paul R. Schulman, *Large-Scale Policymaking* (New York: Elsevier, 1980), who closely examines the Apollo project.
12. Charles E. Lindblom, "Who Needs What Social Research for Policymaking?" *Knowledge: Creation, Diffusion, Utilization* 7, no. 4 (June 1986): 345–366, at p 362.
13. For others, see Ronald D. Brunner, "Conceptual Tools for Policy Analysis," paper presented at the annual meeting of the American Political Science Association, Chicago, September 3–6, 1987.
14. William Ascher, "The Use of the Developmental Construct in the Policy Sciences: Examples from International Relations and Latin American Politics," paper presented at the annual meeting of the American Political Science Association, Chicago, September 3–6, 1987.
15. Leonard Saxe and Michelle Fine, *Social Experiments: Methods for Design and Evaluation* (Beverly Hills, CA: Sage, 1981); and David H. Greenberg and Philip K. Robins, "The Changing Role of Social Experiments in Policy Analysis," *Journal of Policy Analysis and Management* 5, no. 2 (Winter 1986): 340–362.
16. Not that these are lacking. See Stuart Hill, "Lumpy Preference Structures," *Policy Sciences* 19, no. 1 (July 1986): 5–32; and Amitai Etzioni, "Making Policy for Complex Systems: A Medical Model for Economics," *Journal of Policy Analysis and Management* 4, no. 3 (Spring 1985): 383–395.
17. Harold D. Lasswell and Abraham Kaplan, *Power and Society* (New Haven: Yale University Press, 1950), pp. x–xi.
18. William Ascher, "Editorial: Policy Sciences and the Economic Approach in a 'Post-Positivist' Era," *Policy Sciences* 20, no. 1 (April 1987): 4; emphasis in original.
19. As suggested in Ascher, "Editorial."
20. See Murray Edelman, *The Symbolic Uses of Politics* (Urbana: University of Illinois Press, 1976); Murray Edelman, *Political Language: Words That Succeed and Policies That Fail* (New York: Academic Press, 1977); Gunnel Gustafsson, "Symbolic and Pseudo Policies as Responses to Diffusion of Power," *Policy Sciences* 15, no. 3 (April 1983): 269–288; and Ronald D. Brunner, "Key Political Symbols: The Dissociation Process," *Policy Sciences* 20, no. 1 (April 1987): 53–76.
21. Harold D. Lasswell, "The Policy Orientation," in Daniel Lerner and Harold D. Lasswell, eds., *The Policy Sciences* (Stanford, CA: Stanford University Press, 1950), p. 11. Also Harold D. Lasswell, "The World Revolution in Our Time," in Harold D. Lasswell and Daniel Lerner, eds., *World Revolutionary Elites* (Cambridge, MA: MIT Press, 1965).

22. Tomas Bertelman et al., *Resources, Society, and the Future* (Oxford: Pergamon Press, for the Swedish Secretariat for Futures Studies, 1980), p. 19.
23. See Peter deLeon, "Futures Studies and the Policy Sciences," *Futures* 6, no. 6 (December 1984): 586–593.
24. William Ascher, "The Evolution of the Policy Sciences: Understanding the Rise and Avoiding the Fall," *Journal of Policy Analysis and Management* 5, no. 2 (Winter 1986): 365–373; at 372.
25. Nor are theirs isolated incidents; see Yehezkel Dror, "Required Breakthroughs in Think Tanks," *Policy Sciences* 16, no. 3 (February 1983): 199–226, for a broad-ranging assessment.
26. Ascher, "Editorial"; Douglas Torgerson, "Between Knowledge and Power: Three Faces of Policy Analysis," *Policy Sciences* 19, no. 1 (July 1986): 33–60; and Brunner, "Conceptual Tools for Policy Analysis."
27. Torgerson, "Between Knowledge and Power," pp. 34, 35, and 35, respectively; emphases in original.
28. Brunner, "Conceptual Tools for Policy Analysis," p. 5.
29. William Barrett, *The Illusion of Technique* (New York: Anchor Books, 1979), pp. xix and 233, respectively.
30. Edith Stokey and Richard Zeckhauser, *A Primer for Policy Analysis* (New York: Norton, 1978), in their classic presentation of technical models, offer only one piece of advice for analytically treating contextual complexities, "Practice" (p. 6).
31. See Donald A. Schon, *The Reflective Practitioner* (New York: Basic Books, 1983), chap. 2.
32. Schon, *Reflective Practitioner*, p. 345.
33. Rein, *Social Science and Public Policy*, p. 212.
34. For an operational attempt, see the analysis of Head Start by Frank Fischer, "Critical Evaluation of Public Policy," in John Forester, ed., *Critical Theory and Public Life* (Cambridge, MA: MIT Press, 1985), pp. 231–257.
35. Lindblom, "Who Needs What Social Research for Policymaking?" p. 361.
36. E.g., see Jurgen Habermas, *Knowledge and Human Interests* (Boston: Beacon Press, 1971); and Jurgen Habermas, *A Theory of Communicative Action*, vol. 1 (Boston: Beacon Press, 1984).
37. As described by Torgerson, "Between Knowledge and Power," pp. 45–51.
38. The Berger Commission Report is quoted in Torgerson, "Between Knowledge and Power," pp. 45–46.
39. Described in a Habermasian framework by Roy Kemp, "Planning, Public Hearings, and the Politics of Discourse," in Forester, *Critical Theory and Public Life*, pp. 177–210.
40. Martin Shubik and Paul Bracken, "Strategic War: What Are the Questions and Who Should Be Asking Them?" *Technology in Society* 4, no. 2 (1982): 155–179. Public awareness of and involvement

in these issues is a point emphasized by Peter deLeon, *The Altered Strategic Environment* (Lexington, MA: Heath, 1987), chap. 5.
41. Rein, *Social Science and Public Policy*, p. 22.
42. Giandomenico Majone, "Technology Assessment and Policy Analysis," *Policy Sciences* 14, no. 2 (June 1977): 174.
43. Most presciently, Harold D. Lasswell, "The Political Science of Science," *American Political Science Review* 50, no. 4 (December 1956): 961–979; and Garry D. Brewer, "The Policy Sciences Emerge: To Nurture and Structure a Discipline," *Policy Sciences* 5, no. 3 (September 1974): 239–244.
44. Alvin Toffler, *Future Shock* (New York: Random House, 1970).
45. Claus Offe, *Contradictions in the Welfare State* (Cambridge, MA: MIT Press, 1984).
46. Hardly an easy assignment; see Kaufman, *Time, Change, and Organizations*.
47. Barbara Tuchman, *The March of Folly* (New York: Knopf, 1984), p. 4.
48. George W. Downs and Patrick D. Larkey, *The Search for Government Efficiency* (New York: Random House, 1986), elaborate. This is not the place to examine the validity of the private sector efficiency thesis; for the moment, let me, with the support of Downs and Larkey and Laurence E. Lynn, *Managing the Public's Business* (New York: Basic Books, 1981), suggest that it is an arguable proposition and worrisome model for public policymaking.
49. Herbert A. Simon, "Rationality as Process and a Product of Thought," *American Economics Review* 68, no. 2 (May 1978): 12; also his "Human Nature in Politics: The Dialogue of Psychology with Political Science," *American Political Science Review* 79, no. 2 (June 1985): 293–304.
50. Rein, *Social Science and Public Policy*, p. 123.

INDEX

A

Aaron, Henry J., 85*n*29, *n*37, 89*n*84, 91, 101*n*1, 103*n*22, 107, 119*n*8
abortion issue, 2, 38, 109
academics, 15–16, 17, 23, 93; vs. public officials, 33
Acheson, Dean, 82, 89*n*88
Acland, Henry, 102*n*9
advice: combined with consent, 90–91, 106; defined, 9, 52
Agnew, Spiro, 65–66, 86*n*45
AIDS epidemic, 40, 77
Aid to Families with Dependent Children (AFDC), 31, 32, 60
Air Force, 58, 59, 63
American Economics Association, 27
American Political Science Association, 19
Amy, Douglas J., 50*n*96, 88*n*80
Anderson, James E., 108, 120*n*11
Anderson, Oscar E., Jr., 44*n*23
anthropology, 22
Apollo project, 108, 120*n*11
Applied Psychology Panel, 57
applied research: "on applied social research," 22; empirical, 16–17, 20; function of, 26; integrated, 27
Arabs, 69
arms: control issue, 114; race, 2
Arnold, Matthew, 1, 10
Ascher, William, 6, 11*n*11, 12*n*13, *n*18, 44*n*20, 45*n*36, 87*n*57, 89*n*84, 103*n*25, 109, 120*n*14, *n*18, *n*19, 121*n*24, *n*26
Ashford, Douglas E., 43*n*7
Association for Public Policy and Management, 27
atomic bomb, 73
Atomic Energy Commission (AEC), 21, 45*n*23, 59, 68
Averch, Harvey A., 88*n*71

B

Bacon, Sir Francis, 15
Ball, George, 64
Baram, Michael S., 51*n*104
Baran, Paul A., 50*n*95, 88*n*79
Bardach, Eugene C., 49*n*82, 50*n*85
Barrett, William, 102*n*9, 112, 121*n*29
Barton, Allen H., 87*n*67
Bauer, Raymond A., 47*n*52
Baxter, James P., 84*n*14
Bay of Pigs, 55
behavioralism, 20, 112
Bentham, Jeremy, 15
Berger Commission, 113–114
Berman, Paul, 34
Bernard, Chester, 20
Berstein, Barton J., 89*n*90
Bertelman, Tomas, 121*n*22
Betts, Richard K., 64, 85*n*42, 86*n*44
Bhopal, 115
black Americans, 7, 61
Blum, John Morton, 84*n*13
Booth, Charles, 17, 43*n*8
Boucher, William I., 24, 46*n*41
Bozeman, Barry, 27, 47*n*56
Bracken, Paul, 88*n*76, 114, 121*n*40
Bray, Charles W., 84*n*14
Brendel, John E., 119*n*4
Brewer, Garry D., 11*n*13, 13*n*29, *n*31, 29, 48*n*67, *n*69, 83*n*5, 102*n*9, 103*n*23, 115, 122*n*43
Brodie, Bernard, 64, 86*n*43
Brookings Institution, 20, 59
Browne, Angela, 48*n*69, 50*n*89
Brown v. *Board of Education*, 60, 99
Brunner, Ronald D., 12*n*13, 102*n*16, 112, 120*n*13, *n*20, 121*n*26, *n*28
budget cuts, 35
Bulmer, Martin, 43*n*8, 87*n*67, 96, 102*n*13
Burke, Edmund, 15